When the Bishop Comes to Visit

An Activity Book for All Ages

By Brook H. Packard
Illustrated by Barbara Desrosiers

Morehouse Publishing
NEW YORK · HARRISBURG · DENVER

Morehouse Publishing, 4785 Linglestown Road, Suite 101, Harrisburg, PA 17112

Morehouse Publishing, 19 East 34th Street, New York, NY 10016

Morehouse Publishing is an imprint of Church Publishing Incorporated.
www.churchpublishing.org

Cover design by Laurie Klein Westhafer
Typeset by Rose Design

Library of Congress Cataloging-in-Publication Data

A catalog record of this book is available from the Library of Congress.

ISBN-13: 978-0-8192-2915-1 (pbk.)

ISBN-13: 978-0-8192-9311 (ebook)

Printed in the United States of America

Dedicated in Memory of the Life and Ministry of
The Rt. Rev. Jim Kelsey
Bishop, Diocese of Northern Michigan (1999–2007)

Contents

Introduction

The idea for this book can be seen entirely in Section 3—a children's companion booklet to a confirmation liturgy. A while back I was the director of family ministries at a modest church outside New York City. The parish demographic of children under six was quite high and the bishop expected for confirmation that year had a reputation for interpolating many anecdotes, hymn snippets, and personal parables into his sermons. Entertaining and illuminating for those over twelve, but difficult to enjoy for parents of active young children!

I put together a teaching coloring book for that day and it not only occupied young children, allowing their parents to listen to the sermon, it was used prior to the bishop's visitation as a reference for the confirmands. I was delighted when Sharon Ely Pearson had a vision to expand what I had initially constructed, turning it into a book about the role of a bishop in The Episcopal Church that went beyond confirmation.

In September 1999, my husband, George Packard, was elected a bishop in The Episcopal Church during a meeting of the House of Bishops. At the time, his official title was Suffragan Bishop of the Armed Services, Healthcare, and Prison Ministries. Originally, this was the chief pastor for Episcopal chaplains in the military, federal prisons, veterans' hospitals, as well as one of the chaplains who served Ringling Brothers' Circus.

Prison Ministries was under the umbrella of this office and included programs for the many who have taken on the important work cited by Jesus in Matthew 25:36. His episcopacy also included Micronesia and Guam, where there are four Episcopal churches and St. John's School. In addition to being "bishop of everything except the kitchen sink," there were programs and conferences for chaplains deployed overseas as well as the 18,000 plus Episcopalians who worship on or near military bases around the world. As the years unfolded, he cared and strategically planned care for the unprecedented: pastoral care at Ground Zero after 9-11-01, along the Gulf Coast after Katrina in 2005, with reservist and full-time military chaplains and their families during the wars in Iraq and Afghanistan. Increasingly, post-traumatic stress disorder became part of his ministry. When he retired in 2010, his title had changed to Suffragan Bishop for Armed Services and Federal Ministries.

For eleven years he got on Metro North's commuter train dressed in collar and clerical shirt and went to The Episcopal Church Center at 815 Second Avenue in Manhattan. When he wasn't commuting he was on a plane somewhere, building relationships and working behind the scenes to make sure the families of chaplains were cared for as well.

After twenty years of going to church and volunteering as a musician and educator, I usually only encountered a bishop during coffee hour, and he or she was focused on the rector, the vestry, or occasionally on the confirmands. Before George was consecrated a bishop, I never saw a bishop outside of a confirmation visitation.

My friends and I (despite being sincere believers, and never having really met a bishop) had our notion of holders of that office shaped primarily by Monty Python or Peter Cooke in *The Princess Bride*. When I told a musician friend who was playing at our wedding that the bishop was coming to give the sermon, he asked, "Should we all wear cardboard boxes on our heads in solidarity?"

Witnessing the work of my husband and a number of his brother and sister bishops dispelled the irreverence I had previously held. It was from being present that I learned the work of a bishop could truly be that of Team Apostle—encouraging and inspiring rather than ordering people about. Holding the words of Matthew 25 foremost was the most powerful way to "guard the faith, unity, and discipline of the Church" (Book of Common Prayer, p. 517). The nature of the episcopacy he served was that Team Apostle is nimble and portable—words I remember my husband using as a theme during a 2003 chaplain's conference shortly after the invasion of Iraq and Afghanistan. Exposure to chaplains and their families taught me a lot about actively following Jesus.

In retirement, it is clear that some of those promises made at his consecration are more prevalent in our lives than others, such as the promise to "defend those who have no helper." Today when he is invited for a confirmation, the relationship begins weeks before the liturgy; he contacts the confirmands, prays for them, and listens to their joys and concerns.

This book is an opportunity to demystify the work of a bishop, grounded in simple, but honest, theology and historical precedence. Institutional churches are going through a rafter-shaking transition right now. Many seminarians I've spoken to observe that—like our dependency on fossil fuels—the system is unsustainable. Does that mean there will be no more bishops or priests? That's unlikely. The more I study the role of bishops, the more I realize they are vital—a connecting rod among dispersed faithful. However, their roles will change, as will the roles of presbyters. Leadership will be the responsibility of every believer, and gifts will no longer be on a checklist handed out at the end of an adult forum.

I am reminded of the time when I reaffirmed my baptismal vows. I was facing an exciting but daunting transition in my own life too. The Archbishop of Perth muttered under his breath as he laid hands on me, "Splendid!"

It is my hope that this book educates in the true sense of the word: eliciting leadership and action from all who read it.

Brook Packard
All Saints Day 2013

How to Use This Book

When the Bishop Comes to Visit was written to clarify and identify the complex and nuanced work of a bishop. There is a significant amount of text on the foundations of discipleship, the role of bishops in history, and the unique polity of The Episcopal Church. The bishop is ultimately the unifier through relationships. When we all understand that we are in relationship with each other, the Church can continue to evolve in a meaningful way.

This book is meant to be interactive. Adults can guide younger readers through the concepts and the vocabulary—some of this information is sophisticated! Words included in the Glossary appear in italics the first time they are used in the text. Teachers may use it in preparation for a lesson during the weeks leading up to a bishop's visitation (whether it be for confirmation or not), or it can be used as the centerpiece of a curriculum for older elementary-aged or middle school-aged children. For those using *When the Bishop Comes to Visit* as a resource in the classroom, focusing on more process-oriented activities will allow students to internalize concepts, making the informational pieces more meaningful.

When an activity is simple, such as drawing or coloring, I cannot recommend strongly enough that adults and older children join in together. God speaks to us in play—maybe even more than in study. It is my hope that a more creative, playful approach to Christian formation be incorporated in all age groups.

Conversely, activities that seem beyond the understanding of young children, such as the *examen*, are not out of their reach at all. Spending time with a young child and exploring prayer together is sacred. The Holy Spirit is sure to be with you in those times.

Section 1 can be used for family discussion and as a resource for confirmation or Church School classes.

Section 2 can be extracted and used as a "countdown" in the weeks prior to the visitation with copies made available to families in the parish.

Section 3 can be duplicated for distribution during a bishop's visitation that includes Confirmation. This chapter repeats some of the material in the earlier chapters, and the language is for younger children as it is designed to be accessible to families who might be visiting a church just for that day. "Get to Know Your Bishop" (p. 47) would make for an informative supplement to the handout. Also be sure to have colored pencils or crayons available to accompany its distribution.

SECTION 1
Where Do Bishops Come From?

First Things First—Let's Meet Jesus

You may have heard stories in church that begin, "There was once someone who did such amazing things and said such wonderful things that people followed him." And if you have not heard that particular phrase, you probably know whom that story is about or who told that story.

Write out the letters of that person's name.

_____ _____ _____ _____ _____

Here is how you can say "Jesus Loves Me" in sign language.

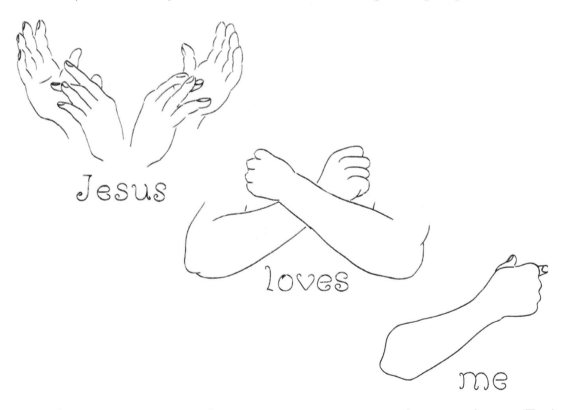

Jesus

loves

me

Practice this sentence and you can pray it quietly anywhere. To know something well, teach it to someone else.

Names of Jesus

Since Jesus' name is known all over the world, there are many ways to write, speak, and pray his name.

See if you can find names for Jesus in other languages.

```
C R H T H Y V S J S T Z U R H
P S C J R C L W U S E I D V E
P W F U E U S I J S G W I J E
E D K R I S T U S D E T H A S
G H E S U K R I S T O E F M A
T Z F Y M E B J A Z H Q J Z M
X I B F O K C I D S E Y W G R
F C Z X X G K C Y Z I H J F Y
N E P E V P M M P B C R F J M
Q Q G O J X B S J Z Y Y F E E
Y C H R I S T O V E C H B Z P
H Y U S E G S U S C E A Y U Q
M G D D I H R S U Z N Z I S A
V U A X U H Y E S H U A L N E
J J F A S H F O I F O Z Y L T
```

(AL) MASEEH	Arabic	(JESUS) CHRISTO	Spanish
GESU	Italian	(JESUS) KRISTUS	Swedish
HESUKRISTO	Filipino	JEZI	Haitian Creole
ICYC	Ukrainian	JEZUS	Polish
IESU	Welsh	JISU	Fijian
ISA	Turkish	JOSHUA	Alternative
ISUS	Bosnian/Croat	YESHUA	Hebrew
JEESUS	Finnish		

Singing About Jesus

Jesus is so much more than a name that we write out, sign, or discover in other languages. Jesus is God. Jesus is friend. We can see Jesus—or the Christ within—in everything around us. Meeting and knowing Jesus is done through prayer, play, helping others (service), and knowing deep inside that every one of us is a child of God.

This spiritual works well with percussion—finger snapping, clapping, foot tapping, shakers, or pencils on a desktop.

> If anybody asks you who you are, who you are, who you are,
> If anybody asks you who you are, just tell them you're a child of God.
>
> If anybody asks you who he is, who he is, who he is,
> If anybody asks you who he is, just tell them he's a child of God.
>
> If anybody asks you who she is, who she is, who she is,
> If anybody asks you who she is, just tell them she's a child of God.
>
> If anybody asks you who we are, who we are, who we are,
> If anybody asks you who we are, just tell them we're all children of God.

The music is written out below. Don't worry if you can't read music, or find someone to help read it, or you can even make up your own melody.

Child of God

Jesus Then

One of the ways we understand more about Jesus is to read the stories about him in the *Second Testament* (also referred to as the New Testament) of the Bible.

Jewish tradition considers a boy to be a young man (adult) at the age of twelve. That tradition continues today with bar mitzvahs for boys and bat mitzvahs for girls acknowledging the transition from childhood. In Jesus' time, a law required that every adult Jewish male who lived near Jerusalem go to that holy city for Passover. This story from the Gospel of Luke is an indication of how eager Jesus was to study and discuss the *Torah*, the book of the *First* or *Hebrew Testament*.

> *Now every year his parents went to Jerusalem for the festival of the Passover. And when he was twelve years old, they went up as usual for the festival. When the festival was ended and they started to return, the boy Jesus stayed behind in Jerusalem, but his parents did not know it. Assuming that he was in the group of travelers, they went a day's journey. Then they started to look for him among their relatives and friends. When they did not find him, they returned to Jerusalem to search for him. After three days they found him in the temple, sitting among the teachers, listening to them and asking them questions. And all who heard him were amazed at his understanding and his answers. When his parents saw him they were astonished; and his mother said to him, "Child, why have you treated us like this? Look, your father and I have been searching for you in great anxiety." He said to them, "Why were you searching for me? Did you not know that I must be in my Father's house?" But they did not understand what he said to them. Then he went down with them and came to Nazareth, and was obedient to them. His mother treasured all these things in her heart. And Jesus increased in wisdom and in years and in divine and human favor.* (Luke 2:41–52)

Can you imagine being so excited about something you're learning that you forget the time and to go home with your family? Mary probably thought Jesus was with Joseph since the women traveled separately from the men in those days. Joseph probably thought that Jesus was with Mary. When Jesus returned home, Luke tells us that Jesus then "*went down to Nazareth with them and was obedient to them. But his mother treasured all these things in her heart. And Jesus grew in wisdom and stature, and in favor with God and man.*"

God speaks to us through our interests and what excites us. Consider what you truly love to do. Is it talking with friends and family? The strategy of playing a game? Sports? Caring for pets? Reading? Making art, poetry, or music? Making others feel at ease? Every one of us is part of the Kingdom of Heaven and can find clues for God's plan for us by paying attention to the things we genuinely love to do.

There is a practice called an *examen*. The word "examination" derives from this Latin root and was the basis for spiritual reflections by St. Ignatius. Cut out the box on the next page and keep it next to your bed. Before going to sleep, you can go through the *examen* process and discover how God is working in your life and Jesus is with you. It is a great way to "put the day to bed" and look forward to a night of deep rest.

The Examen

1. Allow yourself to breathe and invite the Holy Spirit to help you look over your day. If your memory of the day seems a bit cluttered or confused, pray for clarity.

2. Go over the day with gratitude. In the company of God, observe what gave you happiness and satisfaction. Whose company did you enjoy? What work was satisfying or challenging? What did you eat, see, feel, hear, and do? God is there with you throughout.

3. Observe your feelings—negative and positive. Is God trying to say anything to you through those feelings? Observe all things—big and small. God is in the details.

4. Ask the Holy Spirit to show you one thing that you can pray and reflect on. It could be a feeling of peace, an image, or a good laugh with a friend. It could also be a feeling of concern for a friend or an issue. A prayer will flow from this reflection. You can use the acronym ACTS to remember types of prayers: adoration, confession, thanksgiving, and supplication. Or you can remember that there are four things we should say to God every day: Wow! I'm Sorry, Thank You, and Please Help. (If you are praying with someone else, you can pray the confession/I'm Sorry prayer silently—this is between you and God.)

5. Pray for a good night's sleep, dreams, healing, and insight from the Holy Spirit. Pray that you are refreshed with hope, strength, and love when you wake up in the morning. You can also ask the Holy Spirit to guide you to answers to any concerns in your sleep.

The Lord's Prayer

As Jesus grew older, he continued to think deeply about the Torah. As he traveled he used it in his teaching and preaching. His disciples and thousands of people who wanted to hear what Jesus had to say followed him.

One of his most famous teaching moments is when he said this about prayer:

> And whenever you pray, do not be like the hypocrites; for they love to stand and pray in the synagogues and at the street corners, so that they may be seen by others. Truly I tell you, they have received their reward. But whenever you pray, go into your room and shut the door and pray to your Father who is in secret; and your Father who sees in secret will reward you . . . for your Father knows what you need before you ask him.

> Pray then in this way:

> Our Father in heaven, hallowed be your name. Your kingdom come. Your will be done, on earth as it is in heaven. Give us this day our daily bread. And forgive us our debts, as we also have forgiven our debtors. And do not bring us to the time of trial, but rescue us from the evil one. (Matthew 6:5–13)

This teaching, preaching, and prayer from Jesus is something we use and do every single day. When we pray the prayer above in Episcopal churches together, we hear "Now let us pray as Christ the Lord taught us. . . ." This is a most important prayer, so let's pause and consider it.

Under each phrase, write or discuss what that means to you personally, how you understand its meaning. Can you rephrase it in words that are more personal?

1. Our Father in heaven

2. Hallowed (holy) be your name

3. Your kingdom come, your will be done on earth as it is in heaven.

4. Give us today our daily bread.

5. Forgive us our debts, as we also have forgiven our debtors.

6. Lead us not into temptation but deliver us from evil

You can put each phrase on an index card. Take a different one each day and think about how the Lord's Prayer is being acted out in your family's life, at school, or at church.

Jesus Today

In those days after the resurrection, Jesus came to visit his friends. He taught and even cooked a meal for them. After forty days, he ascended into heaven, but remains with us as more than a memory. At Pentecost, Jesus sent the Holy Spirit to be our comforter and inspiration. While we may not be able to see Jesus today, we know he is with us.

When we serve him in spirit, we can sense Jesus' presence.

We can get to know Jesus through prayer and particularly by being open to the people the Holy Spirit brings to us every day. The Holy Spirit is that helper Jesus said would bring his memory alive again so much so that it is vivid and real.

Many people ask: "What would Jesus do?" Some wear bracelets with the abbreviation "WWJD" as a reminder. Another question we can ask ourselves, particularly if someone is being very difficult, is: "What if this person *was* Jesus?" or has some part of Jesus we can't see right away. What is Jesus up to right now in my life? What is the invitation? When we seek to meet Jesus every day, we grow into our best possible selves.

If your day is just beginning, take a moment to pray that you have open eyes, ears, heart, and mind to meet Jesus. If this is the end of the day, go over what you did from when you got up to when you started getting ready for bed. Was there an opportunity to meet Jesus?

Using the blank beads on the bracelet below, write in ways you can meet and serve Jesus.

The Great Commission

We know the stories from and about Jesus through four books of the Bible that we refer to as "The Gospels." These are the stories passed on by communities who followed Jesus' teaching in the early church. The four books are Matthew, Mark, Luke, and John. Three of those books tell the story known as the Great Commission. It is an important summary Jesus left for us to do. And it is an assurance. Here it is from the book of Matthew:

> *Go therefore and make disciples of all nations, baptizing them in the name of the Father and of the Son and of the Holy Spirit, and teaching them to obey everything that I have commanded you. And remember, I am with you always, to the end of the age.* (Matthew 28:19–20)

The story of the Great Commission is found in Mark, chapter 3, verses 13–19, and Luke, chapter 6, verses 12–16. If you want to be a real scholar, see *how* these stories are different and wonder *why* they might be different. You may want to draw a picture of what you imagine that moment was like when Jesus spoke these words.

People who followed Jesus very closely: they lived and shared food together, as well as his teaching and healing. They stepped out in faith and love every day. They were known as his *disciples*, meaning students or learners. At some point the disciples became known as *apostles*. Apostle means "one who is sent." They took what they had learned and became the teachers. The twelve apostles we know in the Bible are specific people.

Draw a line in both directions from the name of each of these followers to a word that describes who they were and what they did:

Listen   DISCIPLE   Follower

Pray   Learner

Learn   Evangelist

Teach   Witness

Worship   APOSTLE   Pupil

Seek peace   Companion

Share   Apprentice

Travel with Jesus   Teacher

                                                                 Adherent

Following Jesus, Jesus Now—The Risen Christ

The historical Jesus has become the risen Christ who is present through God's Spirit. No matter how old we are, we can all be followers of Jesus once we have **met** him. We can be disciples and apostles even at the same time. We can live each day with our senses open to God's will for us as learners, teachers, creators, and just being ourselves.

Some think the apostles became Apostles ("Team Apostle") when Jesus commissioned them. Others think it happened on the day of Pentecost. Whenever it happened, their way of thinking and being began to change. See how many people were deeply affected on that first day of Pentecost:

> *So those who welcomed his message were baptized, and that day about three thousand persons were added. They devoted themselves to the apostles' teaching and fellowship, to the breaking of bread and the prayers. (Acts 2:41–4)*

Before followers of Jesus were called **Christians**, those who were changed by Jesus' work said they followed **The Way**. Christianity started with communities of children, adults, and elders, bound together by fellowship, the breaking of bread, service, and in prayer. Many lived together, sharing possessions and helping each other. Today we call that "mutual aid" because people realize that a community is strongest when it cares for the weakest members.

One of the reasons the Good News (Gospel) of Jesus spread was that each of those twelve Apostles went out and traveled; teaching and sharing so that even more people would know Jesus' message of love and justice.

Write about or draw one activity you did today that was the activity of a disciple or an apostle.

Team Apostle

James   Judas   James   Matthew   Bartholomew   Simon   John   Thomas
Jude   Philip
Andrew   Peter

Investigate those who were on the first Team Apostle. Where did each one travel? What did each one teach? Team Apostle continues today and includes bishops, priests, deacons, and you and your friends. Draw faces on the more recent members of Team Apostle.

Grow with Team Apostle

Paul's letters (*epistles*) record that he was a member of Team Apostle: encouraging, advising, and evangelizing. The Good News of Jesus and his teachings quickly spread due to the work of people like Paul.

Many study bibles include maps of Paul's travels. You may want to investigate the places he traveled to and which routes he took to get to them. Read the epistles to see what Paul's concerns and hopes were for each of these communities.

Try this activity to see how Christianity grew exponentially. You will need a lot of room to draw and write for this activity. Have on hand something like a roll of plain paper, or chalk on a chalkboard or sidewalk before you begin.

1. At the far left of your writing space, draw a picture representing Paul.

2. To the right of Paul, starting at the top of the writing space, write this list of places we are certain Paul visited:

   - Rome
   - Corinth
   - Galatia
   - Ephesus
   - Philippi
   - Colossae
   - Thessalonica

3. We're going to be guessing a little here because we want to show how something can increase exponentially. Suppose each of those seven locations has only one church with 100 followers. Next to each location, draw a box with the number 100 written in each one.

4. Let's continue to imagine a little. Suppose three people in each church told one person who really began to understand and love Jesus. Draw three lines—maybe like a fan—out from each of those seven boxes.

5. Draw three boxes next to each of those three fans. You should now have 63 boxes. We're being very conservative and assuming that only three people told others the Good News. It would have been more likely that each of those 63 boxes represents a new house church with at least 25 people coming to worship and share. In just three exchanges of this little activity, we can see that 1,575 people had their lives changed in probably less than a year.

Paul traveled for many years, visiting more places than the seven listed above. He was not the only one spreading the Good News. There were twelve members of Team Apostle traveling and teaching. The 3,000 who began to follow Jesus on the Day of Pentecost could not have kept the life-changing experience of knowing Jesus to themselves. This is the kind of growth that cannot be written out on a roll of paper—someone would have to write a computer program to count the numbers.

The Early Church

The story of bishops begins in the Bible.

Remember those 3,000 people who changed their lives on that first Pentecost? They couldn't keep this new way of living to themselves. Each one told others about it, they then told others, and the communities began to grow and spread all over the world they knew. This was also due to the hard work of Team Apostle.

When we look at the early church, we recognize that the language used in the part of the world where Christianity was born was Greek. Many of the words we use today—in church and outside of church—come from Greek roots. Knowing the history of the words helps us understand their deeper meanings.

Ekklesia, for example, means "the gathered" or a community of believers. Ekklesia also means "church," but not church as a building or a place to "go to." The church really is the people gathered, figuring out or *discerning* God's will for their lives.

As the early church—the gathered communities of those following The Way—grew, they needed a leader to help them. The Greek word for a leader of a community is *presbyteros*, which is now interpreted as presbyter or priest. These kinds of leaders are not like officers in the military, but more like teachers. Their role is to encourage and bring out the best in the people in a particular faith community.

Still, the early Christians needed ways to connect with each other. They realized that as they went beyond their immediate location and built relationships with other communities in this new growing family of churches, an overseer was needed: someone who could visit the different communities, listen and participate in what was going on, share information, and help them out. The Greek word for overseer is *episkopos*. It also means to visit, to look into someone's needs with the intention of helping him or her. Episkopos in English nowadays means "bishop."

Say the word "ē-p̆ı-skōp-ōs" out loud. What word are you reminded of when you hear the four syllables? What words are you reminded of when you say the third syllable? It is the same root of the words microscope and telescope and gives us an important clue as to the role of a bishop.

Draw a line between the Greek word and its matching word in English.

Mono   Deacon

Ekklesia   One

Presbyteros   Beginning (first letter of the alphabet in Greek)

Episkopos   Thanksgiving

Diakonos   End (last letter of the alphabet in Greek)

Eucharist   Church/The Gathered

Alpha   Leader/Presbyter/Priest

Omega   Christian love, love in community

Agape   Overseer/Bishop

Apostolic Succession—Historic Episcopate

Team Apostle was—and still is—very busy! The Episcopal Church is one of a number of churches that considers their bishops, priests, and deacons to be part of a tradition that is over 2,000 years old. That tradition is called *Apostolic Succession*. It is believed that the authority to teach about The Way was transferred from the original Apostles through the laying on of hands by Jesus.

The laying on of hands is an ancient tradition in many religions. It is real as well as symbolic, a Jewish sign of blessing inherited by the early church. When we do things with purpose or *intention*, that activity is changed for the better. This could include preparing a meal, touching a friend to comfort him or her, or even doing your homework to prepare for better understanding.

When a bishop in The Episcopal Church is consecrated, brother and sister bishops lay hands on the new bishop as one bishop says this prayer as they surround him or her:

> *Therefore, Father, make (this person) a bishop in your Church. Pour out upon him/her the power of your princely Spirit, whom you bestowed upon your beloved Son Jesus Christ, with whom he endowed the apostles, and by whom your Church is built up in every place, to the glory and unceasing praise of your Name.* (Book of Common Prayer, p. 521)

The laying on of hands has been going on for centuries. It is referred to as Apostolic Succession when it occurs during an *ordination* or *consecration*. But the intentional laying on of hands can happen anywhere at any time. It is another way to communicate caring in a relationship. The laying on of hands occurs during baptisms, confirmations, blessings, healing prayers, and other times when we ask God to cover this moment with presence and assurance.

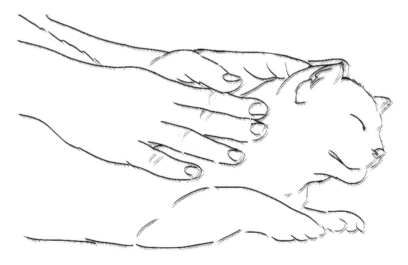

The First Bishops

During the *Apostolic Age* the leaders in the church were those who knew Jesus personally and were commissioned to spread the Good News. We can guess that each of the apostles met and trained natural leaders and commissioned them to continue with the teaching and the breaking of the bread, laying their hands on the next generation of apostles as they asked for God's covering.

It is important to remember some of the Greek words that have been handed down to us. Ekklesia means "the gathered," so when the word "church" is used we are talking about a community of people meeting in someone's home. Today there are many Christians who meet in house churches. Some choose to live together in community, just as the early followers of The Way lived.

Those with titles in the early church were deacons or bishops. In a house church, there would be at least one person designated as deacon (*diakonos*) and responsible for service to those in need in the community. The house church usually met in the home of the bishop (*episkopos*). In that gathering place, people worshiped and shared meals, and goods like clothing and food were distributed. The bishop and his home were the center of community relationship. The terms presbyter (priest or elder) and episkopos were interchangeable.

> *Now during those days, when the disciples were increasing in number, the Hellenists complained against the Hebrews because their widows were being neglected in the daily distribution of food. And the twelve called together the whole community of the disciples and said, "It is not right that we should neglect the word of God in order to wait on tables. Therefore, friends, select from among yourselves seven men of good standing, full of the Spirit and of wisdom, whom we may appoint to this task, while we, for our part, will devote ourselves to prayer and to serving the word." What they said pleased the whole community, and they chose Stephen, a man full of faith and the Holy Spirit, together with Philip, Prochorus, Nicanor, Timon, Parmenas, and Nicolaus, a proselyte of Antioch. They had these men stand before the apostles, who prayed and laid their hands on them. (Acts 6:1–6)*

This is a description of an early church community solving a problem together. There was some division in that particular community—the Jews who had adopted the ways of the Greek world (called Hellenistic Jews) felt that their widows were not being treated fairly. The passage also describes how this community discerned the sharing of responsibilities. We can see the beginnings of the necessity for a unifier to be part of the organization of The Gathered.

Have you experienced something similar in your family, school, camp, or church? Remember that we share love, food, sorrows, and joys. Read Acts 4:32–37 for another description of the organization of the early church.

Is there one phrase that moves or really pops out at you? On a separate piece of paper, write it out as creatively as you can. Decorate the letters, draw a picture, praying as you write and draw.

Christianity Spreads and Grows

In 325, after his conversion to Christianity, the Roman Emperor Constantine allowed followers of Jesus to practice their faith. Now the early church could meet in public buildings. Sometimes those buildings were temples dedicated to other gods and taken over by Christians.

Bishops were needed in different ways now. Christianity was spreading for many reasons. Not only were the teachings and practices of Jesus good news, but a number of early Christians were merchants and traveled around the Mediterranean. Hospitality—a value inherited from Middle Eastern culture—was an important virtue for all travelers. For Christians, it meant wherever they traveled they could experience fellowship and a community far from home. Hospitality was not just a virtue in a bishop, but a duty.

Those early communities were dedicated to sharing and mutual aid. Church funds were available to travelers as well as the poor. But it is human nature to be preoccupied with one's self (which is why Jesus taught about forgiveness and grace), so bishops were to take charge should there be questions about receiving and dispersing community funds.

The mutual aid that was possible in a small community became very difficult to manage as the church spread out over larger and larger areas. The work of a pastor and evangelist—both cornerstones of Jesus' command in the Great Commission—were not so simple to execute. The visit and "scope" parts of the word episkopos became very important.

ACTIVITY: Mutual Aid

Develop the part of yourself that is an episkopos. Put together an investigative kit of some paper and something to write with, and possibly something with which to record a conversation. Check in on someone in your family and ask them how they're doing. Offer to help them through prayer, a helping or kind touching hand, a treat, or just a visit.

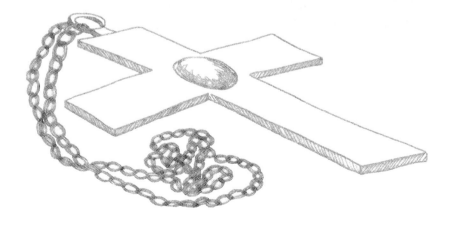

Famous Bishops of Long Ago

St. Nicholas was probably the Bishop of Myra (part of modern-day Turkey) and lived from 270–343. It is said that Nicholas's wealthy parents died in an epidemic and that he gave away his entire inheritance to help the poor. He was raised by his uncle, also named Nicholas, who was the bishop of Patara, also in Turkey.

There are many legends about St. Nicholas and associated miracles during his life and after his death. Once he became bishop he continued to share his wealth with the poor. One famous legend has Nicholas throwing bags of gold into the windows of young women who needed help. He lived in tumultuous times for Christians. In the days before Constantine declared Christianity the religion of the Roman Empire, Nicholas spent time in prison. In 325, Nicholas attended the First Council of Nicea with other bishops to discuss the faith. His feast day is December 6.

St. Patrick was a missionary Bishop of Ireland, 387–460. He is known as the Patron Saint of Ireland. Born in Great Britain, the stories say he was kidnapped at the age of 16 and brought to Ireland as a slave. During those years, Patrick worked as a shepherd, which is lonely work. He used those days on the hillside to talk to God. Patrick escaped, became a priest, then a bishop, and returned to Ireland to do the work of Team Apostle.

There are many legends about St. Patrick. He used the shamrock to teach about the Trinity. We still worship with a prayer known as St. Patrick's Breastplate (*The Hymnal 1982*, #370 and interpreted as "Peace Before Me," *Wonder, Love, and Praise*, #791). St. Patrick's feast day is March 17.

Bishops Today Around the World—The Anglican Communion

There are three religions that derive from the story of Abraham in the book of Genesis: Judaism, Christianity, and Islam. Jews, Christians, and Muslims are all part of a very large family that can claim Abraham as the great, great, great (just keep saying "great" until you can't say it any more) grandfather of our faiths.

Within the enormous family of the Abrahamic faiths, there are smaller families. Those who know and follow Jesus as God's son are part of a family known as Christians. There are millions of Christians around the world, and hundreds of *denominations*—smaller families. These families differ in the way the Jesus' teaching is interpreted.

The Episcopal Church is a member of the Anglican family. The Anglican Family around the world is known as the *Anglican Communion*. This family has 85 million cousins in 165 countries.

The central office for the Anglican Communion is in London. The Archbishop of Canterbury is the head bishop of The Church of England and is considered to be the symbolic head of the Anglican Communion. There have been Archbishops of Canterbury since 597 when Augustine of Canterbury was appointed "Apostle to the English." Every ten years—on years ending in the numeral 8—the bishops of the Anglican Communion gather to discuss issues concerning the Church at a gathering called the Lambeth Conference.

The highest concentration of Anglicans is in countries on the continent of Africa. The most common instrument for worship in the Anglican Communion is a drum. Many Anglicans worship outside.

Choose a song that has its origins from the continent of Africa from the list below. Using percussion instruments—handmade works great—interpret it in your own way with family, friends, or your Church School class.

The Hymnal 1982:   602: Jesu, Jesu, fill us with your love
Wonder, Love, and Praise: 783, Hallelujah! We sing your praises!
                                   787, Siyahamba (We are marching in the light of God)

The 2008 Lambeth Conference was themed around an African method of Bible study. Each bishop in attendance received a copy of the worship and Bible study guidelines as well as the hymnal, *Lambeth Praise*, which has contributions from the musical traditions of all the churches in the Anglican Communion. Write a letter to your bishop asking to borrow the Lambeth resources for exploration and study for your church.

During Sunday morning worship, listen for "the Anglican cycle of prayer" during the prayers. You will hear the names of places that are part of the Anglican Communion.

Coming to America

The Episcopal Church is uniquely American in its *genesis*. Even though it shares similar worship and structure with The Church of England and the greater Anglican Communion, its evolution was greatly influenced by the young democracy that was going to become the United States of America.

When people from England immigrated to the eastern shores of North America, they brought their faith with them. God was a constant in an unknown, foreign land. Some were members of The Church of England. They needed priests and overseers. Having a helping overseer 3,500 miles away, who had to travel two months across the Atlantic Ocean on a dangerous voyage, was not practical at all. A bishop's task of cultivating relationships when the colonists' experience was so very different from life in England would be very difficult.

There was also the matter of identity for the church. The Anglicans that came to the colonies had a strong desire to worship in their unique way as well as agree on rules, leadership, prayer books, *doctrine*, and *mission*.

Those Anglican colonists were challenged during the Revolutionary War. There were even instances of Anglican priests who were killed for their loyalty to the Crown. Most colonists were fighting to separate themselves from England's tyranny, and this particular community of believers was part of The Church of England. In those days, priests had to go to England to be ordained and swear an oath of loyalty to King George.

After the Revolutionary War, the Anglican Church in America began to reorganize itself in a way more fitting to the young nation that was to become the United States. That included changing the name to The Episcopal Church. It was important to some who contributed to shaping The Episcopal Church that there be bishops and Apostolic Succession. This made it unique from other *Protestant*, more *Congregationalist* denominations in the colonies and eventually, the United States.

The shield of The Episcopal Church reminds us of this history. The colors red, white, and blue are the colors of the flags of both the United States and England. The blue field in the upper left corner has nine smaller crosses, which form an "X" shape. These nine crosses represent the nine dioceses that met in 1789 to form the early Episcopal Church. The "X" shape represents the cross of St. Andrew, which is on the flag of Scotland (see page 24 for the significance of Scotland).

Color in the red and blue parts of The Episcopal Church shield.

The Early Episcopal Church

One important difference between The Church of England and The Episcopal Church is how the idea of democracy affected the structure of the church. The Episcopal Church **elects** its bishops from its membership while the Church of England **selects** its bishops by an appointed committee.

The colonists fought and sacrificed enormously to break away from England and its *monarchy*. Not everyone organizing The Episcopal Church wanted Apostolic Succession or bishops to have roles similar to the ones they had in England. The debate can be divided roughly by geographical location: colonists from New England supported a more hierarchical church than those from Virginia and parts of the south. It was debated intensely; those who wanted Apostolic Succession and bishops serving as overseers won the debate.

This presented a bit of a problem for newly elected American bishops: bishops who were part of the unbroken generational chain of Apostolic Succession and could convey that through the laying on of hands were across the Atlantic, in England. The English bishops were forbidden by royal law to ordain or consecrate anyone who wouldn't take an oath of loyalty to the monarchy.

The solution was for the first bishops to go to Scotland—which had itself been something of a colony of England. There was an Episcopal Church of Scotland, complete with bishops. Those bishops did not have to adhere to royal law, as the king determined that the "official" religion of Scotland would be Presbyterianism. So while the Scottish bishops didn't have any official support, they also didn't have to follow the royal rules.

The first bishop to be consecrated was Samuel Seabury (1729–1796). Seabury was not the first to be elected, however. There were some who were elected at the same time but did not have the money to pay for the voyage to Scotland and could not leave their families, farms, or businesses. It is ironic that Seabury goes down in history as the first American bishop of The Episcopal Church. He was a solid supporter of King George, a chaplain for the King's American Regiment. However, after the war he did not move to England but remained in Connecticut and was loyal to the new democratic government.

Others followed Seabury to be consecrated across the sea. Soon there were enough bishops in The Episcopal Church to continue the chain of Apostolic Succession/ Historic Episcopate without the necessity of an Atlantic voyage.

The Episcopal Church: Beginnings and Bishops

Across

4 Bishops in The Episcopal Church are chosen in an . . .

6 The Episcopal Shield has a cross that represents this apostle, the patron saint of Scotland

7 The word that describes a country ruled by a king or queen

8 Church of England priests had to swear an oath of allegiance to this person

10 Many colonists wanted a bishop who was part of the unbroken chain of _____ Succession

11 The country to the north of England where the first bishop of The Episcopal Church traveled to get ordained/consecrated

12 Members of The Church of England are all considered . . .

Down

1 The country where priests went to be ordained before the formation of The Episcopal Church

2 Before the Revolutionary war people in the "New" World, America, settled in . . .

3 What Christians do when they gather on Sunday morning

5 The word that follows "Anglican" when we think of the greater family to which Episcopalians belong

9 Number of dioceses that met in 1790 to form The Episcopal Church

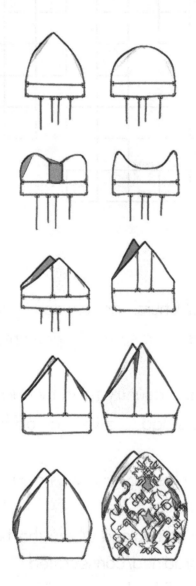

Throughout history, the hats that bishops wear have changed!

Polity = How We are Governed

Since 1789, The Episcopal Church has evolved, responding to the culture around it. The basic structure remains, strongly influenced by the same founders who had a vision of democracy in the United States.

Like the United States, The Episcopal Church has a *bicameral* governing body. The United States has the House of Representatives and the Senate, while the church has the *House of Deputies* and *House of Bishops*. These legislative bodies meet every three years at *General Convention*.

Each diocese appoints up to four clergy and four lay leaders as participants in the House of Deputies. Just as each state in the growing union of the United States has equal representation, it was important to those in 1789 that every diocese have equal representation. The House of Deputies has grown from the first Convention, from 44 deputies to over 900 (including alternates) today. They generate, discuss, and vote on resolutions—policy that affects The Episcopal Church.

The House of Bishops is composed of those who have been elected bishop. The House of Bishops meets separately from the House of Deputies during General Convention. During the course of Convention, you will see runners with booklets of legislation going between both gatherings as legislation gets revised, discussed, and revised again before a vote. Both houses must agree on legislation in order for it to be adopted.

The resolutions from General Convention are published and made available to every church online or in the form of a book. These are not arbitrary rules and laws, but positions that define the identity and mission of The Episcopal Church. They represent the agreements necessary for larger church relationships.

General Convention is held for legislative process, but it also becomes a gathering of the entire Church. Since 1789 it has contributed to the formation of an Episcopal Church identity. The daily worship displays a variety of music, language, and art. It is hard work for the deputies and bishops, but there is also a celebration of the extended family coming together.

ACTIVITY: The Episcopal Church in Action

1. Go to the web site *www.generalconvention.org/gc/resolutions*
2. In the upper right part of the page is a search field. Type in an issue and hit the search button.
3. Resolutions—proposed and resolved—will come up for you to download and read.
4. Find one that you can discuss with your friends or Church School class.

Parents and teachers reading this with younger children may want to search for The Children's Charter for the Church and discuss how your church welcomes younger members of the community.

The House of Bishops

Up until the twentieth century, bishops were priests of congregations with all the responsibilities that come along with those positions. Periodically, they would meet to share ideas, concerns, resources, and for fellowship. These days, bishops are no longer directly responsible for local church life and have more freedom to attend national and international gatherings.

In addition to General Convention, the House of Bishops meets twice a year—usually in March and September—for four to six days. One of those meetings is held at an Episcopal Church conference center, such as Camp Allen in Texas or Kanuga in North Carolina. For the other annual meeting, there is a host bishop and diocese that practices the hospitality known in the church since its early days.

When the House of Bishops gathers, the bishops pray, worship, discuss, learn, and plan. As the chief liturgical officer in an episcopacy or diocese, bishops are introduced to a range of music and prayer that are both new and tap into the tradition of Anglican worship. They also listen. When the bishop comes to visit your church, she or he will be bringing all these experiences and resources along as well. There are new hymns, prayers, and interesting ideas about how other regions of The Episcopal Church worship or engage in education, outreach, and mission. Sometimes, a word from another country can change the way Eucharist or education is discussed and explored.

ACTIVITY IDEAS: Beyond Your Church

- Write down a question you might like to ask the bishop about something new he or she has learned when the House of Bishops met. Can it be shared with your parish during the visitation? Is there a resource the bishop can send on to your parish after the visitation?

- Research Episcopal Church Conference Centers like Kanuga and Camp Allen. See what they have to offer, what the program calendar might be. Research retreat locations in your diocese. If the location or program offerings seem appealing, see if you can plan a family, Church School class, or even a whole church retreat there.

- Consider starting a group about faith among your friends. You can share books, movies, or activities such as cooking or sports and games. The best way to find ideas is to get together with some food, say a prayer asking for guidance, and let the ideas flow.

Provinces and Dioceses

The Episcopal Church in the Americas has over two million active members (2011). Membership spans all the way from Maine to Oregon, Haiti, Taiwan, Micronesia, and countries in Central and South America. One bishop couldn't possibly oversee that many baptized persons living all over the world! The Episcopal Church is broken down into smaller sections.

There are nine large geographic areas in the United States called *provinces*. Each province is divided up into *dioceses*. There are a total of 111 dioceses in The Episcopal Church.

Province 1	7 dioceses
Province 2	11 dioceses, including Haiti
Province 3	13 dioceses
Province 4	20 dioceses
Province 5	14 dioceses
Province 6	8 dioceses
Province 7	12 dioceses
Province 8	19 dioceses, including Taiwan, Navajoland, and Micronesia
Province 9	7 dioceses (Central and some countries in South America)

When a province gets together, it's like a HUGE family reunion, with cousins, second cousins, great-great uncles and aunts. A diocese is a little like a reunion with just cousins, and your home church is like your immediate family. Most—but not all—bishops oversee geographical dioceses.

Find out who is in your larger church family. Start with the province, then the diocese. Always remember that there is a larger family called the Anglican Communion and an even **larger** family of followers of Jesus.

ACTIVITY: Provinces and Dioceses

With a red crayon, color in your diocese. With a yellow crayon, color all the dioceses (areas) you have either lived in or visited.

With a dark-colored crayon or marker, make a dot for friends or family who live in other provinces and dioceses.

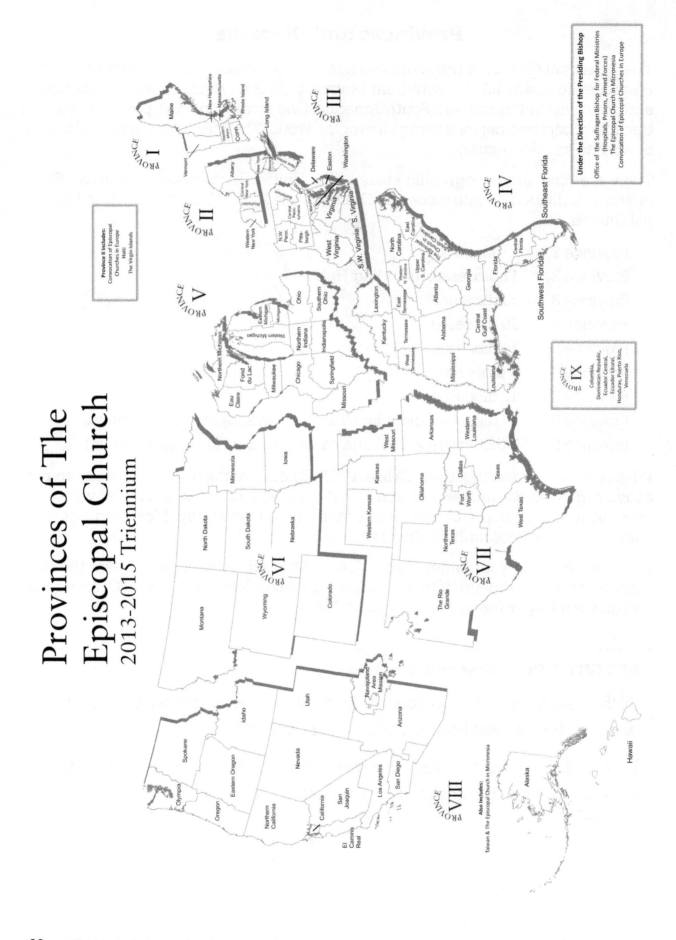

Provinces of The Episcopal Church
2013-2015 Triennium

PROVINCE I

PROVINCE II

Province II Includes:
Convocation of Episcopal
Churches in Europe
Haiti
The Virgin Islands

PROVINCE III

PROVINCE IV

Under the Direction of the Presiding Bishop

Office of the Suffragan Bishop for Federal Ministries
(Hospitals, Prisons, Armed Forces)
The Episcopal Church in Micronesia
Convocation of Episcopal Churches in Europe

PROVINCE V

PROVINCE VI

PROVINCE VII

PROVINCE VIII

PROVINCE IX

Colombia,
Dominican Republic,
Ecuador Central,
Ecuador Litoral,
Honduras, Puerto Rico,
Venezuela

Also Includes:
Taiwan & The Episcopal Church in Micronesia

Province I
Maine, New Hampshire, Vermont, Massachusetts, Western Mass., Rhode Island, Conn.

Province II
New York, Albany, Central New York, Western New York, Rochester, Long Island, N.W. Penn., Pittsburgh, Bethlehem, Central Penn.

Province III
Washington, Easton, Delaware, Virginia, S. Virginia, S.W. Virginia, West Virginia, Maryland

Province IV
North Carolina, Upper S. Carolina, Western N. Carolina, East Carolina, The Episcopal Church in South Carolina, East Tennessee, West Tennessee, Tennessee, Kentucky, Lexington, Alabama, Central Gulf Coast, Mississippi, Louisiana, Georgia, Atlanta, Florida, Central Florida, Southwest Florida, Southeast Florida

Province V
Ohio, Southern Ohio, Indianapolis, Northern Indiana, Chicago, Springfield, Milwaukee, Fond du Lac, Eau Claire, Michigan, Eastern Michigan, Western Michigan, Northern Michigan

Province VI
North Dakota, South Dakota, Nebraska, Minnesota, Iowa, Montana, Wyoming, Colorado

Province VII
West Missouri, Missouri, Kansas, Western Kansas, Oklahoma, Arkansas, Western Louisiana, Dallas, Fort Worth, Texas, West Texas, Northwest Texas, The Rio Grande

Province VIII
Spokane, Olympia, Oregon, Eastern Oregon, Idaho, Nevada, Utah, Arizona, Navajoland Area Mission, Northern California, California, El Camino Real, San Joaquin, Los Angeles, San Diego, Alaska, Hawaii

Bishops Serve in Many Ways

Bishops who are elected to serve in a geographical diocese have a *jurisdiction* and are usually (but not always) associated with a cathedral. The cathedral is a place to worship but may include offices from where the bishop and his or her staff can fulfill their promises in action. There are times when the bishop must be a decider, make legal decisions, and use his or her authority to discipline.

There are 112 geographical dioceses and over 300 active bishops in The Episcopal Church. Is one of those bishops visiting your church soon?

Episcopacies

We can say our faith is grounded in prayer and action, but how we choose to serve Jesus has no fence or border—it cannot be put on a map. There are bishops who cultivate relationships with priests and baptized persons with no connection to a geographical area. These bishops serve *episcopacies*. Maybe one of these bishops is coming to visit your church. That is very exciting because that bishop is close to how the first Team Apostle served the early church.

Examples of bishops with special *pastoral* responsibility:

The Bishop Suffragan of Armed Services and Federal Ministries supports Episcopal priests who are *chaplains* in the military, including those who are on active duty and supporting men and women in combat, chaplains in veterans' hospitals, and chaplains in prisons and churches around the world on military bases in which over 18,000 Episcopalians worship.

Convocation of American Churches in Europe—The bishop who oversees these congregations in Europe has a cathedral for an office in Paris, France. There are eight churches in the Convocation, but the episcopacy also supports mission churches, education projects, Episcopalians with a house church in Kazakhstan. The bishop for the Convocation used to be appointed by a special committee, but in 2001 the Convocation elected its own bishop.

The Bishop Suffragan for the Office of Pastoral Development is a bishop to the bishops. For this bishop, the "your people" that he or she promises to serve are other bishops.

Suffragan Bishop

The Church uses the term "suffragan" to designate supporting bishops. These are bishops who make the same promises as other bishops. Even though suffragan means supporting, there are Suffragan Bishops responsible for many faith communities in local dioceses. Does your diocese have a Suffragan Bishop?

Bishops Who Help Bishops

Assistant Bishop

A diocesan bishop can appoint an Assistant Bishop. The Assistant Bishop is someone who is already a bishop but who has no current responsibilities. The Assistant Bishop must be approved by the Standing Committee of the diocese and serves at the behest of the current diocesan bishop until that bishop retires.

Assisting Bishop

Occasionally a diocesan bishop has need for some temporary help so he or she asks another bishop to assume the position of Assisting Bishop. This position gives the diocese more Episcopal presence, but unlike an Assistant Bishop this position has temporary—but significant—standing.

Bishop Coadjutor

The Latin root of coadjutor is co-assister. Usually when a bishop gives notice for retirement, there is an election for a new bishop so that someone is ready to take over the duties of the retiring bishop. The Bishop Coadjutor will work with the current bishop until his or her day of retirement and then assume the position of bishop.

Presiding Bishop

Every third General Convention—every nine years—the bishops elect a Presiding Bishop. Around the year 2000, The Episcopal Church adopted the language of the Anglican Communion to refer to its Presiding Bishop as Primate for international reference.

The Presiding Bishop used to be the bishop with the most *seniority* who presided over meetings when bishops got together. He was the bishop in a diocese or episcopacy who took on the role of Presiding Bishop, making sure the meetings stayed on topic and the order of business was discussed in an effective way. In 1919 the role of Presiding Bishop was changed. Now the Presiding Bishop is a minister of connections. He or she serves as a Chief Pastor, the Primate representing The Episcopal Church at primates' meetings, chairs Executive Council meetings, and visits dioceses and provinces. In 2006, The Episcopal Church elected its first female Presiding Bishop.

```
B  P  I  R  N  D  I  O  C  E  S  E  C  V  O
E  S  O  L  V  G  A  U  K  F  B  F  T  W  N
N  R  E  A  B  K  T  E  V  R  H  O  N  V  B
O  P  R  E  S  I  D  I  N  G  O  Y  O  N  M
I  K  R  A  E  S  A  S  S  I  S  T  I  N  G
T  P  D  S  E  L  I  P  L  K  W  A  T  H  H
C  C  C  U  P  Y  W  S  U  S  L  L  A  R  Z
I  P  Z  F  I  N  N  Y  T  P  B  D  C  O  O
D  H  K  F  S  P  T  N  A  A  A  L  O  M  I
S  S  E  R  C  T  F  H  F  F  N  N  V  M  S
I  I  M  A  O  F  C  V  A  T  B  T  N  P  R
R  R  C  G  P  A  O  D  N  Z  Z  D  O  D  L
U  A  A  A  A  S  J  L  K  R  P  Q  C  G  H
J  P  Q  N  C  W  C  O  A  D  J  U  T  O  R
P  X  T  U  Y  E  C  N  I  V  O  R  P  X  K
```

ASSISTANT

ASSISTING

CHAPLAIN

COADJUTOR

CONVOCATION

DIOCESE

EPISCOPACY

JURISDICTION

PARISH

PRESIDING

PROVINCE

SUFFRAGAN

The Promises We Make

Bishops are priests who have won an election for bishop. In a diocese, everyone attending the Diocesan Convention can vote for the candidate of his or her choice. Often there are many rounds of voting, as there are more than two or three candidates. The House of Bishops, rather than a diocese, elects bishops who specialize in being pastoral overseers or have a unique episcopacy.

Once someone has been elected bishop, he or she has to be approved by a percentage of the Standing Committee in all of the dioceses in The Episcopal Church. Then there is the ordination/consecration of the newly elected bishop. In these *liturgies* we ask for God's blessing on the new bishop, praying that this person be strengthened in this new job. The laying on of hands in the Apostolic Succession/Historic Episcopate takes place during this liturgy. Two very important components of that liturgy are the examination and promises.

When we join our *ekklesia*—our community of faith—we make promises to God, ourselves, and to each other. We draw upon or invoke the name, memory, and reality of Jesus to help us. For some, parents and godparents make promises on our behalf when we are baptized because The Episcopal Church is one of the denominations in which baptism can occur when we are babies, a time in our lives when we are not capable of understanding those promises.

Before we make our promises in public for everyone in our church to witness, there is an examination. This is not the kind of examination or test for which you study—but you do practice it. It is similar to the *examen* (page 5). There is no grade as this is a process to see how ready we are to make and keep the promises. Those who are committed to following Jesus are asked to examine unseen, but real parts of themselves regularly through prayer, discussion, and holy listening.

Examinations and promises are part of baptism and confirmation. In The Episcopal Church, there are promises made in public by the clergy—the deacons, priests, and bishops. Because a person cannot be elected bishop unless he or she is first ordained a priest (all bishops are priests but not all priests are bishops), most of the promises and examination questions are for those who have made the decision to become priests.

A promise can also be called a *covenant*, which makes it a very sacred promise. The first promises that we say (or were said for us when we were infants) can be found in the Baptismal Covenant. Deacons, priests, and bishops each have an examination that builds upon these first promises, which we all say together whenever we recite the Nicene Creed.

Using the Book of Common Prayer, look at each of the services where these questions are asked of all of us.

- Holy Baptism—pages 304–305
- Ordination: Bishop—pages 517–519
- Ordination: Priest—pages 531–532
- Ordination: Deacon—pages 543–544

Build a Foundation of Faith

All of questions in these blocks are examination questions and promises made by bishops. Many of these questions are also asked (and promised) of everyone who is baptized, confirmed, or ordained a deacon or priest.

Will you guard the faith, unity, and discipline of the Church?	Will you share with your fellow bishops in the government of the whole Church; will you sustain your fellow presbyters and take counsel with them; will you guide and strengthen the deacons and all others who minister in the Church?	Will you be merciful to all, show compassion to the poor and strangers, and defend those who have no helper?
Will you be faithful in prayer, and in the study of Holy Scripture, that you may have the mind of Christ?	Will you boldly proclaim and interpret the Gospel of Christ, enlightening the minds and stirring up the conscience of your people?	As a chief priest and pastor, will you encourage and support all baptized people in their gifts and ministries, nourish them from the riches of God's grace, pray for them without ceasing, and celebrate with them the sacraments of our redemption?

Will you accept this call and fulfill this trust in obedience to Christ?

Are you persuaded that God has called you to the office of bishop?

Will you be diligent in the reading and study of the Holy Scriptures, and in seeking the knowledge of such things as may make you a stronger and more able minister of Christ?	Will you endeavor so to minister the Word of God and the sacraments of the New Covenant, that the reconciling love of Christ may be known and received?	Will you undertake to be a faithful pastor to all whom you are called to serve, laboring together with them and with your fellow ministers to build up the family of God?	Will you persevere in prayer, both in public and in private, asking God's grace, both for yourself and for others, offering all your labors to God, through the mediation of Jesus Christ, and in the sanctification of the Holy Spirit?

Do you believe that you are truly called by God and his Church to this priesthood?

Will you look for Christ in all others, being ready to help and serve those in need?	Will you do your best to pattern your life in accordance with the teachings of Christ, so that you may be a wholesome example to all people?	Will you in all things seek not your glory but the glory of the Lord Christ?
Do you now in the presence of the Church commit yourself to this trust and responsibility?	Will you respect and be guided by the pastoral direction and leadership of your bishop?	Will you be faithful in prayer, and in the reading and study of the Holy Scriptures?

Do you believe that you are truly called by God and his Church to the life and work of a deacon?

Will you continue in the apostles' teaching and fellowship, in the breaking of bread, and in the prayers?	Will you persevere in resisting evil, and, whenever you fall into sin, repent and return to the Lord?	Will you proclaim by word and example the Good News of God in Christ?	Will you seek and serve Christ in all persons, loving your neighbor as yourself?	Will you strive for justice and peace among all people, and respect the dignity of every human being?

Do you believe in God the Father?	Do you believe in Jesus Christ, the Son of God?	Do you believe in God the Holy Spirit?

Color the promises we **all** make in blue (for our baptismal waters).
Color the promises that deacons, priests, and bishops make in red (for the Holy Spirit).
Color the promises that priests and bishops make in green (for growth).
Color the promises that a bishop makes in purple (for a "royal priesthood").
Hint: Start from the bottom up with the blocks to ensure a solid foundation!

The Ministry of a Bishop

The examination questions and promises made are the foundation of the work of a bishop. It is assumed a bishop will persevere in prayer and be diligent in studying scripture, for example, as that will guide the bishop in the work that is to be done. It is also important for all of us to do this kind of interior study. Everyone should listen to God's will for our lives.

The preceding pages have clues about the work of a bishop. In the list below, check off which activity is part of a bishop's and/or priest's *ministry*.

Activity	Bishop	Priest
Cultivate relationship		
Visit		
Extend hospitality		
Oversee		
Teach		
Preach		
Visit		
"Scope" out a community with the intention of helping		
Unify		
Encourage and support through action and liturgy		
Chief liturgical officer		
Chief pastor of the diocese/episcopacy		
Chief evangelist of the diocese/episcopacy		
The Decider—discipline and make legal decisions		

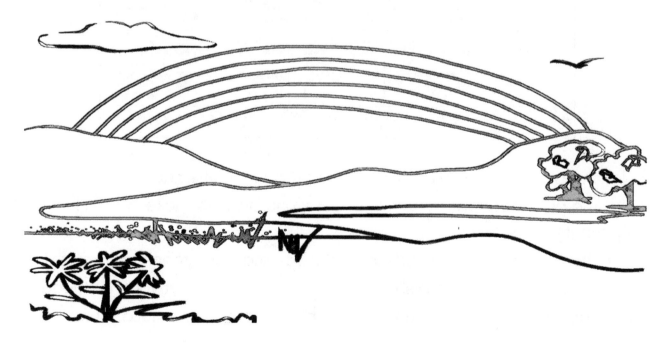

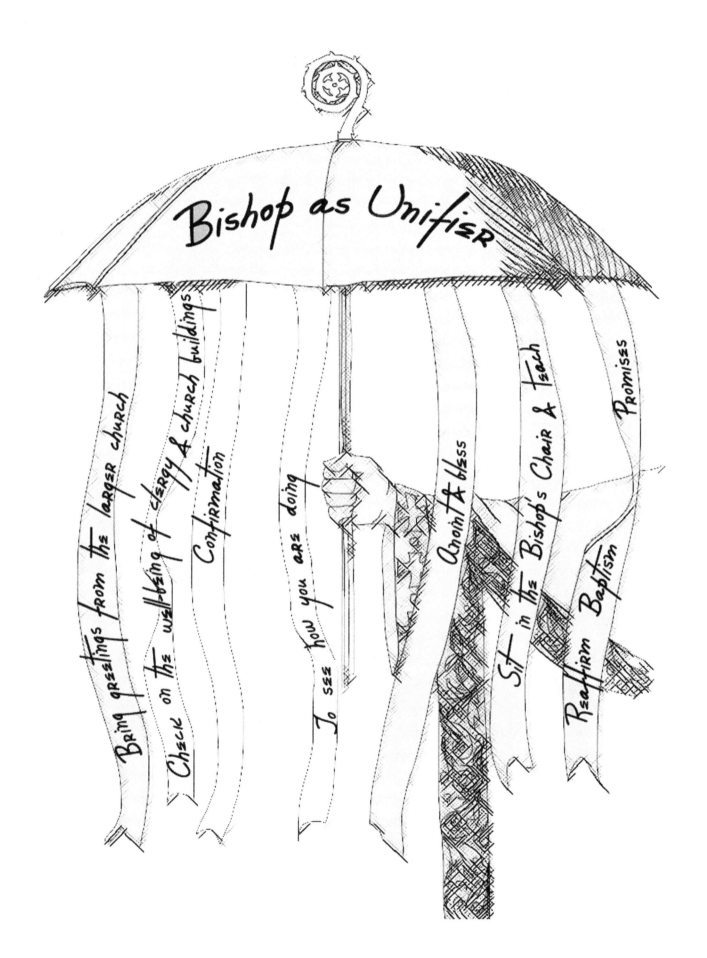

Symbols of the Bishop's Office

There are three items that are symbols of the office of a bishop.

The *crozier*, or staff, is given to a bishop during the consecration and ordination to the episcopacy. It is typically curved at the top and is reminiscent of a shepherd's crook. The crozier dates as far back as ancient Egypt; similarly, the pharaohs carried shaped staffs in ancient times.

Each episcopacy or diocese has a crozier that is different, decorated or carved with images that display the uniqueness of that bishop's responsibilities. The bishop will be carrying the crozier throughout the service in his or her left hand in order to bless with the right hand.

The bishop will be wearing a ring that is unique to the office. The ring dates from the time when letters were sealed with wax. A candle made of a special wax (usually beeswax and resin) was lit, and the wax dripped on the folded letter. A bit of metal (either a stamp or a ring) was pressed into the warm wax, leaving a unique imprint. Bishops use their rings to make an imprint on wax upon the consecration certificate when they are present and participate in the consecration of a new bishop. If you visit your diocese's offices, you may find your bishop's certificate framed and hanging on her or his office wall.

The *pectoral cross* is a cross that is to be worn on the breast. Some bishops choose to wear it in the left-hand pocket of a shirt, close to the heart. Many bishops wear their pectoral crosses all the time as a reminder of Jesus. You will see the cross worn outside the bishop's vestments during the worship. When the bishop is not vested, the chain of the cross is visible.

Vestments

There are many *vocations* that require people to wear a uniform so that they can be identified as someone to go to for help. For example, nurses, firefighters, police officers, and clergy. In addition to referring to clothing, uniform also means "consistent" or reliable.

Vestment is the term used for the uniform of clergy—bishops, priests, and deacons. Many of the vestments we see in churches derive from Roman times during the first few centuries of the early church. The *chasuble*, for example, was outerwear, similar to a poncho. The church retained the use of these traditional garments despite changes in fashion.

There are vestments worn by all priests, and special vestments that identify bishops. If you were to see a bishop grocery shopping, you would never know that person was a bishop unless you could see the chain of the pectoral cross peeking out of a chest pocket.

When the bishop arrives, he or she will not be dressed in full vestments, but you will be able to identify the bishop from his or her purple *clerical* shirt. Priests usually wear black (but some now wear other colors) shirts with a white collar; bishops usually wear purple. There are a few different theories as to why the color purple is associated with bishops:

- It is the color of penitence and reflection, the color used in the church during the seasons of Advent and Lent. As chief pastor in the diocese or episcopacy, the bishop is to remind us that he or she is with us in prayer.
- Purple is traditionally the color of royalty and authority. Purple was a very difficult and expensive dye, reserved for the clothing of Roman senators, kings, queens, and other royalty. Historically, some bishops were perceived as being in positions of power. Since so much of the Church draws on tradition, the color purple remains as a way to identify the bishop as a figure of authority.

You will encounter some bishops who choose to wear black like a priest when they are not on a visitation. Below are two clerical shirts. One is for a priest or deacon and should be colored black. The other is the shirt for a bishop and should be colored purple or magenta. Don't forget to leave the collars white!

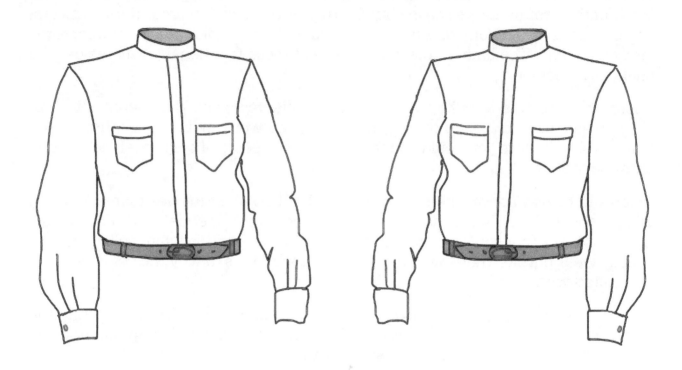

Vestments of a Bishop

A number of vestments are worn by deacons, priests, and bishops. There are a few vestments that distinguish the bishop.

The most distinguishable vestment worn only by bishops is the *mitre*. This hat dates from the time of Jewish high priests. Its points are reminiscent of the flames of Pentecost when the apostles received the Holy Spirit. The two tabs of fabric on the back of the mitre are called *lappets*. It is said that those were sewn on so that when the bishop rode a horse to visit a congregation, the mitre wouldn't fly away.

You may want to draw a cross on the front of this mitre and use a different color for the lappets.

The bishop will be wearing a pectoral cross outside the vestments, the bishop's ring, and walking with the crozier—the three symbols of the office of a bishop. Throughout the worship, the bishop has to remember specific times to take off or put on the mitre, and pick up or put down the mitre. It is a lot to remember!

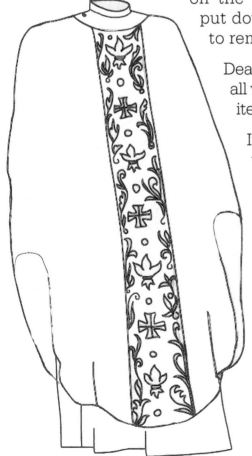

Deacons, priests and bishops all wear a long, white robe called an *alb*. This is another item of clothing which dates from Roman times.

It is very likely that Eucharist will be celebrated when the bishop visits. If that is the case the bishop and the priest will be wearing *chasubles* over their albs. The chasuble will be the appropriate color for the time in the liturgical year.

Here is a picture of an alb with a chasuble over it. Color the chasuble the color for the seasons of Epiphany and Pentecost. (Hint: these are the expansive, growing seasons of the church year. What color do you associate with growth?)

Deacons, priests, and bishops wear *stoles*, scarf-like fabrics that are typically the appropriate color for the liturgical year. Priests and bishops wear them around their necks, hanging down the front of the alb. Deacons wear them over the left shoulder and tucked into a rope belt called a *cincture*.

Color the deacon's stole the color for Pentecost, red.

Color the priest's and bishop's stole blue or purple for Advent.

There are other vestments that the bishop might be wearing depending on the occasion. The bishop might choose to wear a *cope*. The word sounds like the combination of the words "cape" and "cloak," and that describes it well. It is a dramatic garment as it is made of a large piece of heavy, usually ornamental fabric. The cope fastens with a clasp in the front and sometimes has a hood in back. The bishop may wear a cope in procession and a chasuble for the Eucharist. If worn in procession it can be removed at the end of the procession or worn for the Liturgy of the Word.

If the bishop is making a formal visit to another diocese or if there is no Eucharist to celebrate, he or she may wear a purple *cassock*. Cassocks are also worn by priests and deacons, acolytes, choristers, and others participating in the liturgy. Yet another vestment from the days of the early church in Rome, the cassock was worn underneath a toga.

Color this bishop's cassock purple or magenta.

There are three more vestments that are worn by bishops during public, highly ceremonial, and formal occasions such as liturgies at General Convention, the ordination of other bishops, and international gatherings. These vestments are called *rochet*, *chimere*, and *tippet*. (Pronunciation of these three words can be found in the Glossary on pages 71 and 73.)

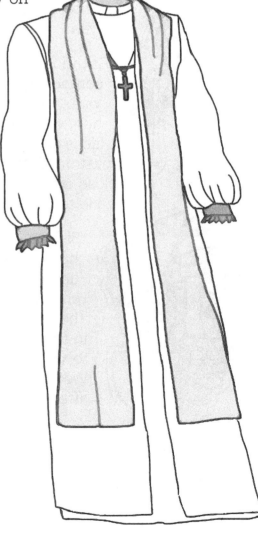

The rochet is put on over a cassock and has long sleeves that could end in ruffles. Over the rochet, comes the chimere—a sleeveless red or black robe. The tippet, a wide, black scarf, goes over the chimere. You might also see your priest wearing a tippet at Morning Prayer or on high holy days instead of a stole.

Color each vestment—the rochet, chimere, and tippet—the appropriate color.

SECTION 2

The Bishop Is Coming!

Why Is the Bishop Coming?

Bishops visit congregations on a regular basis according to the local customs and *canons* (sets of laws). Some diocesan canons state that a bishop is required to visit every congregation in his or her diocese at least once a year. Bishops who cultivate pastoral relationships in non-geographical dioceses must visit all the clergy and the communities that comprise that episcopacy once a year. You can imagine that this could be a tall order for episcopacies that have communities and clergy numbering more than 52—the number of Sundays in a year.

Visitations can be scheduled at the request of a bishop or someone contacting the bishop from the congregation—from the rector, vicar, priest-in-charge, or lay leadership. During that conversation, what is new, exciting, demanding, or challenging in parish life is communicated so that the bishop can truly fulfill his or her pastoral duties. You can also personally reach out to the bishop(s) close by or any you would like to get to know better by writing a letter.

Bishops visit to "scope" out what is going on in the parish, to have conversations; for confirmation; to celebrate; to teach and preach; to encourage; to anoint and bless people, events, chrism oil, and church buildings; and to bring greetings from the greater church family. Some churches have a special day in the liturgical calendar year where the bishop always comes to visit, such as Palm Sunday, the first Sunday in Advent, Ash Wednesday, or their special feast day if their church is named after a saint.

Ask your priest or deacon why the bishop is coming and write the answer on the line below. What questions might you like to ask him or her?

_____

The Bishop and Your Church

The bishop is with your congregation even when he or she is not there on a visit. The bishop has made the promise to be with you in prayer and is in touch with the leadership in your church.

There are signs around your church building that the church is in the care and under the supervision of a bishop. There may be photographs of the bishop or bishops displayed.

Many older churches have a bishop's chair. Historically, the chair is called a *cathedra*, which is Latin for a chair with arms. It is the root of the word cathedral—the location where the bishop does his or her work and the "seat" of a bishop. The cathedra is one of the symbols of the bishop's office. The chair also reminds us of the bishop's role as teacher: there is a tradition of sitting down to teach.

The bishop's chair traditionally was placed in the *apse* of the church, behind the high altar. As church design changed, the bishop's chair was moved to one side—typically the left—of the altar. The bishop is expected to sit in this chair during the worship part of the visitation. In some churches the chair is bolted down, which can make the bishop's participation awkward. The bishop may feel it is impolite to not sit in The Chair even though it doesn't facilitate participation in worship. Newer churches often have a "presider's chair" which can be used by the priest or bishops when they visit.

Your church may also have a window or plaque or other acknowledgment of the bishop. Take some time to look around the church to investigate any reminder that your church is under the bishop's care.

God's Mission = Our Mission

Just as a body, though one, has many parts, but all its many parts form one body, so it is with Christ. For we were all baptized by one Spirit so as to form one body . . . and we were all given the one Spirit to drink. Even so the body is not made up of one part but of many. (1 Corinthians 12:12–14)

As the passage from 1 Corinthians observes, we are one body with a variety of gifts. Bishops and priests have made a promise to work with and encourage all in the baptized in order to build up the family of God, the Body of Christ.

Many congregations take the time to collaboratively write vision and mission statements so they can better clarify their unique roles in the family of God.

A *vision statement* outlines how the parish is to fit into the greater Church—the Body of Christ around the world. A *mission statement* is more practical and outlines how your local church will carry out the work described in the vision statement.

The bishop is directly concerned with the vision and mission of your parish. The bishop may be collaborating or advising the leadership in the parish about what is going well or about what could be improved.

ACTIVITY: What's Your Mission?

Find out if your church has a vision and/or mission statement. If this is the case, write them here. Does your diocese have vision and mission statements? Write those too. What do they have in common? How do they differ?

Get to Know Your Bishop

It's been announced that the bishop is coming. Go through the checklist below and see what you can learn about this visitor and his or her presence in your church already. To learn more about the bishop, you can have someone help you go to your diocese's website or the Internet to find out where the bishop went to school and seminary, the year he or she was ordained a priest, the year the bishop was elected, whether the bishop has a family, and sometimes even what hobbies a bishop has.

☐ Bishop's name _____

☐ Bishop's episcopacy or diocese _____

☐ Date of bishop's visitation _____

☐ Reason for visit _____

☐ Countdown—how many Sundays until the bishop's arrival? _____

☐ Does your church have a bishop's chair? _____

☐ Does your church have a photograph of the bishop displayed? _____

☐ Are there photographs of other bishops? _____

☐ Does your church have a window, plaque, or other signs that it is or has been in a bishop's care? _____

ACTIVITY: Learn More About Your Bishop

If your church hands out paper bulletins for the Sunday worship, a wonderful addition to that bulletin for the visitation would be a profile of the visiting bishop. Using the guideline below, write out a biography for inclusion in the confirmation worship bulletin. Much of the information can be found on an Episcopal Church or diocesan website.

Where was the bishop born?

Where did the bishop grow up?

Was the bishop always an Episcopalian?

Where did the bishop go to college?

Where did the bishop go to seminary?

In what year was the bishop ordained a priest?

In what year was the bishop ordained/consecrated a bishop?

What did the bishop do before he or she was ordained a priest?

Does the bishop have any hobbies?

Does the bishop have a family?

What does the bishop like most about the Episcopal faith?

Does the bishop have a vision of the direction the Church should be taking?

Helping Your Bishop Get to Know You

The bishop is not a guest nor is the bishop a stranger. Your parish community is under his or her Episcopal guidance and care. It's like a family member who needs to travel as part of work. If a mother or a father works as a truck driver, for example, traveling for weeks at a time, and comes home, that person would not be a guest, but a senior member of the household.

The bishop doesn't need a reason such as a confirmation or other special occasion to visit. The bishop can visit when he or she wants—or you invite the bishop. It is important that the bishop doesn't come to your church and then leave with no connection or relationship. Relationship is at the heart of the bishop's promise.

If the bishop is coming for confirmation, it is particularly important that the bishop arrive early to meet with the confirmands and their families. This is a significant moment in their spiritual lives and the bishop will not just want to go through the motions.

The bishop will probably contact the confirmands months in advance, if not personally, through email or telephone calls.

ACTIVITIES:

Make a list of the bishops in your diocese. Are there Assistant, Suffragan, or Assisting bishops? Do any retired bishops live nearby?

Join together with several other companions in church, and if there is more than one bishop nearby, delegate the task of writing a letter to each one. You may want to thank the bishop for his or her service, wish the bishop well with your own prayer of blessing, and tell the bishop something about you and your church, your concerns, joys, and hope. If the diocese to which your church belongs has less than 52 parishes, you can directly ask the bishop to come for a visit. The bishop doesn't have to preach—maybe you'd like the bishop to visit your Church School class and answer questions.

Create an invitation for the bishop to visit using ideas from other celebratory invitations such as for birthdays, anniversaries, or graduation parties.

Make a video for the bishop. It could include songs, questions, jokes, a skit—anything that tells the bishop something about you and your community. The bishop is interested in everyone's gifts and talents.

Getting Ready

Most bishops are traveling every Sunday, visiting. Their "home church" is the greater church. Some may travel a small distance, others may drive for hours, and others may have flown in an airplane thousands of miles and are staying in a foreign land.

The bishop is a traveler who is checking in on your church as a caring pastor who has the authority to guide and provide. It is a unique situation: the bishop is both a guest and a host. You may want to review what you've learned about the bishop and share it with others. If elected recently, the bishop will be doing things that are new to him or her. Is the bishop traveling with his or her family? If so, they are guests in your church and should be shown the gift of gentle hospitality.

Depending on the bishop who is visiting and your individual congregation, some things the bishop might expect are:

- A parking space near the entrance of the church
- Transportation from where the bishop is staying
- Someone to help find a place to have private time for prayer and preparation, vest (get dressed for the liturgy), and show the bishop where the bathroom is located
- Water! Maybe even a light snack
- A meeting with the rector, deacon, choir, confirmands (if the bishop is visiting for Confirmation), sexton and/or verger, or leadership in your church before the worship and a chance to review any pertinent parish journals and records

---

ACTIVITIES:

While the promises made by bishops are all the same, every bishop has a different temperament. For some, the traveling and being "on" for a new parish is difficult. Reflect for a while on what it might be like to always meet new people and be in new environments. Write a prayer for the visiting bishop.

Imagine visiting your home church for the first time. Is it easy to find the bathroom, classrooms, nave, and parish hall? Maybe there's a map of your church displayed prominently. If not, make a map or write directions on how to find everything. Offer this in hospitality to the bishop or to any other travelers.

Find one thing in your church that is special to you. It could be a particular window, a tree outside, a prayer from the Eucharist, or a hymn you love to sing. Make a card for the visiting bishop describing why that is special.

Find out what the bishop looks like! The bishop will probably arrive wearing a purple/magenta shirt, but that's not always a given. This way you can make eye contact and smile to welcome the bishop.

What You Might Expect

No matter why the bishop is coming, expect a longer Sunday morning worship than usual. Just as Thanksgiving Dinner when we enjoy the company of extended family and friends is longer than a weekday supper, the Sunday morning of a bishop's visitation will take some time.

The bishop will not be changing the worship in your congregation even though he or she is the chief pastor. The bishop will respect the customs of your parish just as someone coming to dinner will respect the customs of your home. There may be some new things, however, that the bishop does during the worship. He or she may chant parts of the liturgy instead of speak it, for example.

You can expect a new sermon, written just for the occasion of the bishop's visitation. In it, the bishop will mention your home church, its mission, and concerns and celebrations that are unique to your parish.

The bishop may be traveling with a family. Welcome them with a smile and a handshake if you can. The bishop may also be traveling with a chaplain—usually a deacon—to assist in vesting and in key parts of the liturgy. The chaplain will be focused and might not have time to socialize. Or your church may be asked to provide a bishop's chaplain to assist him or her. This could be a member of the clergy, a lay leader, or an acolyte.

The celebration following the worship is often a little fancier when the bishop comes. It's important to remember that bishops and their families can be as shy as any of us, and that for some temperaments socializing doesn't come naturally or can be very tiring. It's also important to remember that the bishop and his or her family may have special dietary requirements, so please don't insist they try that special cake that everyone in the parish enjoys! Don't take shyness or not eating personally. Don't take it personally if the bishop is tired and needs to leave early or rest—particularly if he or she drove some distance to be with you.

The best thing to do to welcome the bishop is to smile with a light in your eyes. If you have a card or a letter and the bishop seems overwhelmed, just slip it into the bishop's hand. He or she will get back to you.

ACTIVITIES:

Think of at least three things that make you feel at ease when you're visiting and write them down.

Think about other people who travel as part of their vocation, or who travel because they don't have a home. Write a prayer for travelers.

SECTION 3

A Confirmation Service Booklet
for Families

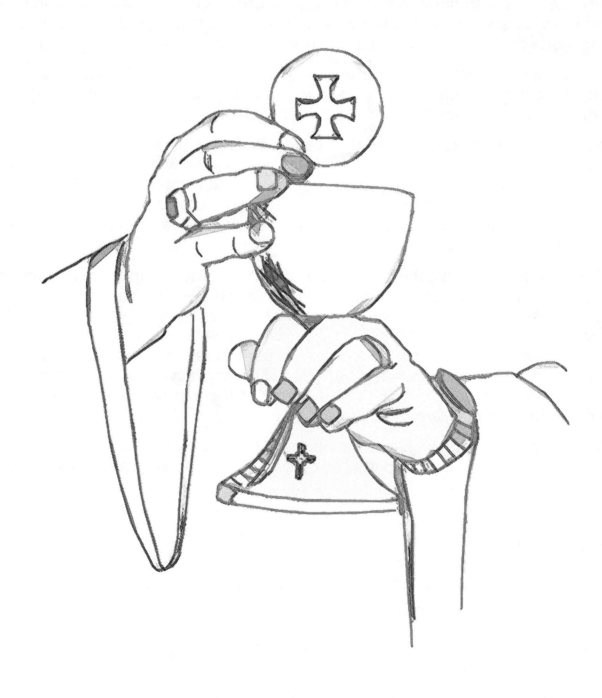

52

Welcome to Our Church!

Every Sunday is special—a day we set aside to pray together, hear God's word while in community, and celebrate with Eucharist. Some Sundays we leave our church joyful, some Sundays we leave very thoughtful about the things God has spoken to us through

our praying . . .

our singing . . .

the pictures, windows, and designs around us.

God also speaks to us through the people gathered together, silences, the sermon, and other sights, sounds, smells, and feelings we have during worship.

How is God speaking to you today?

Today Is Special

This particular Sunday, God may speak to us through what is happening during the worship. People are being confirmed. They have made a very important decision to be part of The Episcopal Church.

Many people are baptized when they are babies.

The adults who care for them promise some important things for these infants. You will hear those promises made again during the confirmation.

Confirmation marks a time when a person is old enough to keep those promises on their own with God's help.

A rainbow is one of the symbols that God keeps promises made to us.

The worship will be very much like other Sundays, except that we have a special visitor who will participate in the worship.

The Church should always welcome strangers as valued guests, but our visitor today is not a guest or a stranger. A bishop is visiting us.

You can't have a confirmation without a bishop!

As the person elected to guide and encourage the faithful in a diocese or episcopacy, the bishop will have some choices in how the worship proceeds. Those places in the worship will be marked with a box that says "Bishop's Choice."

What's a Bishop?

In The Episcopal Church, bishops are elected to oversee an area (diocese or episcopacy), encourage the baptized, and help priests and congregations grow in Christ.

The Bishop will process in at the beginning of the service.

Bishop's Choice: The bishop can choose to carry a crozier. If the visiting bishop has the responsibility of caring for this parish—if this parish is in the bishop's diocese—he or she will probably choose to carry a crozier. It is a special walking stick, a symbol of the bishop's office and geographical diocese.

There is something else about the crozier: it is shaped like a shepherd's staff—the stick the shepherd uses to guide the sheep. Notice the curve or crook in the crozier. The shepherd can use that to rescue sheep that have fallen and need help up. All croziers are a little bit different. They have symbols carved into them that represent something unique about the bishop's office and the people in his or her care.

If the visiting bishop doesn't explain the symbols of the crozier, you can go up and ask after the worship.

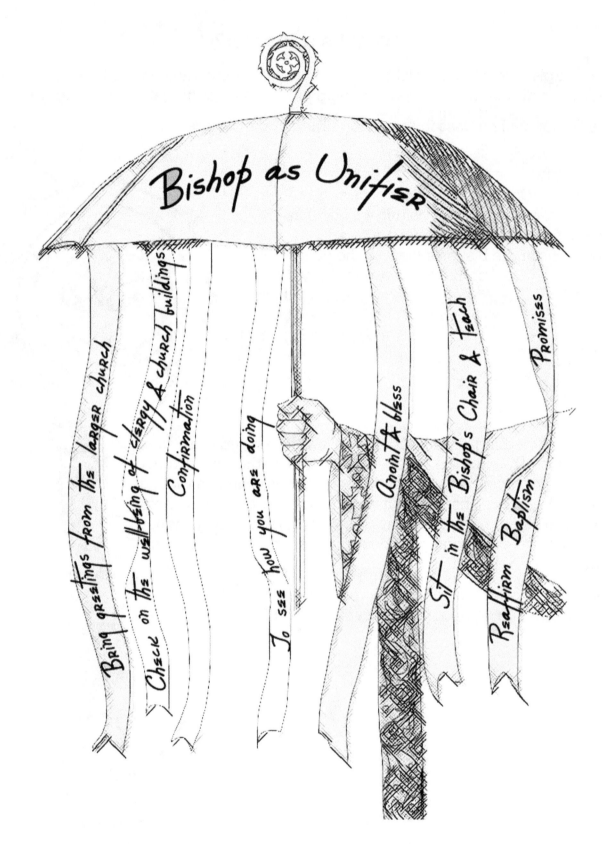

Bishops help unite the faithful through relationships. Today the bishop is visiting for confirmation, but as you can see from this picture, there are many reasons for a bishop to visit your church.

How to Recognize the Bishop

The bishop is also wearing some articles of clothing (vestments) that are different than those worn by the priests, acolytes, and choir members.

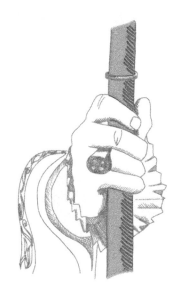

The first thing you may notice is his or her hat. It is called a mitre. A mitre is a very ancient vestment, dating from the time of Jewish high priests. Its points remind us of the flames of Pentecost when the apostles received the Holy Spirit. Bishops are descendants of the apostles.

Do you notice the two tabs of fabric on the back of the bishop's mitre? Those are called lappets and were sewn on so that when the bishop rode a horse to visit a congregation, the mitre wouldn't fly away!

Besides the mitre, the bishop will be wearing two other symbols of the office of the bishop: a ring and a pectoral cross.

Bishop's Choice: Most bishops wear a mitre, but it is not required that a bishop wear one for a confirmation service.

The Service Begins

After the singing of a hymn of praise, when the processional arrives at the front of the nave by the altar, there will be a salutation and greeting led by the bishop.

Bishop's Choice: The bishop will respect the parish traditions when it comes to worship. However, the bishop has choices when it comes to alternatives for prayers and readings from Holy Scripture. The bishop will make those choices based on the alternatives in the Book of Common Prayer, pages 928–929. You can see that the bishop can choose alternatives for the lessons, Psalm, and Gospel.

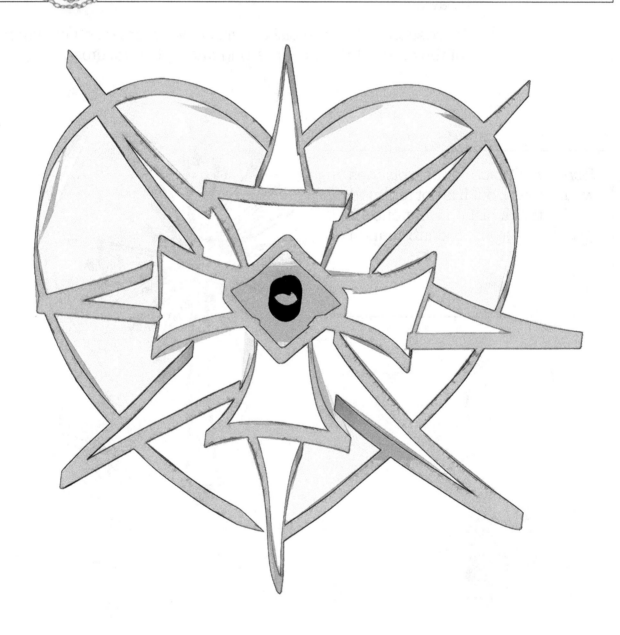

Sitting, Standing, and Teaching

What follows is the First Lesson

Bishop's Choice: Bishops will probably respect the worship pattern and tradition in the parish being visited, but can choose whether the gathered stand or sit. Watch the bishop for cues.

Then those gathered will say or sing a psalm together. In some churches, the choir sings the psalm and the congregants sit and listen. Psalms are prayers shared by Jews and Christians. They may have been written by King David, but are there for all of us.

The most well-known psalm is Psalm 23. You can draw or write something to show what the words of this psalm mean to you.

The Lord is my shepherd, I shall not want.
He makes me lie down in green pastures;
He leads me beside still waters; He restores my soul.

If a word or phrase from the psalm being said today gives you an idea, feeling, or a memory—God is speaking to you. You may want to draw with that in mind.

The Gospel

Before the reading of the Gospel, we usually sing a hymn to prepare our hearts and minds for these stories about or told by Jesus.

Bishop's Choice: The bishop may want to bless the deacon or priest before he or she process out into the congregation to proclaim the Gospel.

The sermon comes next. This week, the bishop will respond to the Gospel in a sermon, giving a special message to everyone who is worshiping—particularly those who are about to be confirmed (confirmands). Listen for what the bishop has to say that addresses the unique character of the community.

What words do you hear?

Draw your own picture of the bishop here.

Bishop's Choice: The bishop can choose to sit or stand during the sermon. If the church has a Bishop's Chair (cathedra), the bishop may choose to preach from that chair.

Sitting and teaching is a time-honored tradition. It is the way that Jesus taught.

Renewing Our Baptismal Promises

Now the confirmands come forward to the front of the nave—usually in front of the altar. Everyone in the congregation stands—not just to be able to see what's going on, but in community support—for the presentation and examination of the candidates. It is time for them to make their promises. These are very much like the promises made for them at their baptism when they were too young to do that for themselves. You can follow along in the Book of Common Prayer on page 415.

Bishop's Choice: The bishop can choose to have the confirmation candidates: 1) respond individually or as a group; 2) stand or kneel; and 3) have prayers for the candidates read by the bishop, clergy, the candidate's parent(s), or someone important in the candidate's life.

The confirmands are presented to the bishop, who asks them some very important questions. This is called an examination. It is not like an examination or test for school, one in which we write out information we've learned from teachers or books. It is an examination of the confirmands' hearts and souls.

When the confirmands have answered truly, they make their promises. We are not only all witnesses to these promises, but we make them again. When the bishop asks us if we will "support these persons in their life in Christ," we need to say as strongly as possible:

We will!

Then we all say what we believe (the Creed) and reaffirm our baptism promises (the Baptismal Covenant). These promises should also be made strongly—and we ask for God's help in keeping them.

I will with God's help.

The Laying on of Hands

Once we have all renewed our promises before each other, the bishop will lay hands on each confirmand's head and say a special prayer. The bishop prays for God's Holy Spirit to empower, sustain, strengthen, and protect each confirmand. We can all pray that prayer for ourselves and for the ones we love, so that we may grow close to Jesus Christ and understand God's will for us in the Kingdom of Heaven—right here on earth!

Bishop's Choice: The bishop may request that parents, godparents, mentors, or spiritual advisors stand behind the candidates with hands on their shoulders during the laying on of hands.

The laying on of hands is a special ritual we do in the Church. Jesus and his disciples laid hands on those who needed strength and healing. When a bishop is made a bishop (consecrated), brother and sister bishops surround the soon-to-be bishop, laying hands on the candidate. This ritual is a Jewish sign of blessing inherited by the early church. It goes back over 2,000 years.

The Peace

Bishop's Choice: The passing of the peace can begin with the bishop exchanging the peace with each candidate and then asking they radiate out through the congregation.

Now we pass the peace together.

A member of the clergy will say: **The peace of the Lord be always with you.**

We respond: **And also with you!**

Then we shake each other's hands or give someone special a hug.

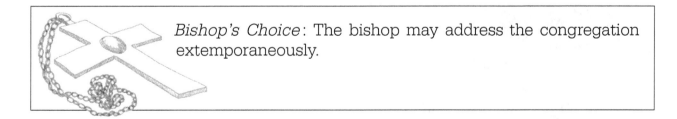

Bishop's Choice: The bishop may address the congregation extemporaneously.

Next is the Offertory. We offer our gifts to God, which includes an offering of music. You can offer your voice and songs to God any time. The Bible tells us to "Sing to the Lord a **new** song!"

You can sing a new song to God every day!

And you can dance a new dance every day!

Draw a picture of yourself dancing and singing!

The Holy Eucharist: Giving Thanks to God

This is exciting because we are preparing for a special meal together or Eucharist, which means thanksgiving. You know what getting the family together on Thanksgiving dinner is like, with turkey, trimmings, shared stories, and love? Well, this is like that and more. We give thanks to God for giving us Jesus and we thank God for bringing us all together.

Bishop's Choice: The bishop is the primary celebrant for Eucharist. With the worship patterns and traditions of the parish in mind, the bishop may choose to chant or not chant this portion of the liturgy; use a form of the Lord's Prayer familiar to the congregation, and use incense.

The bishop will be celebrating the Eucharist, remembering all that Jesus gave and sacrificed for us in love. The bread is broken and blessed.

We are reminded that Jesus broke bread and shared wine through the blessing of those elements, and that Jesus asked us to "Do this for the remembrance of me."

You may want to try to remember Jesus at every meal you have. Not only when you say a blessing for the meal, but as you eat it and enjoy your family and friends. One of the promises of baptism is to "Continue in the apostles' teaching and fellowship, in the breaking of the bread, and in the prayers." God wants us to enjoy our families and friends.

Before we go to the table at the front of the church, we say the Lord's Prayer together. You may want to hold the hands of family that are standing next to you as you pray.

There are many ways to pray about the Eucharist and ways to think about it. Draw a picture of what the Eucharist means for you today.

Thanksgiving

Bread and Wine

The Last Supper

Family meal

Taking Jesus into our hearts

Getting "clean"

Food for our soul

A remembering of Jesus' sacrifice and love

After we have received communion or a blessing, we can go back to our seats and think prayerfully about how God spoke to us in worship. You may want to pray that you remain close to God in your thoughts and actions throughout the week.

Using a pencil, "walk" the labyrinth below, which is an ancient way that people "walked their prayers."

We now say a special prayer of thanks to God for this mystery, which concludes:

**And now, Father, send us out
to do the work you have given us to do,
to love and serve you
as faithful witnesses of Christ our Lord.**

It is time for us to end the worship as a community. You may also want to keep the confirmands in your prayers this week.

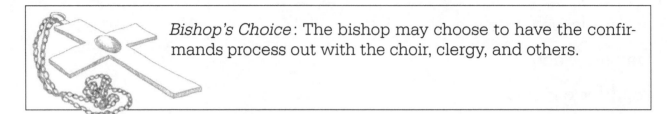

Bishop's Choice: The bishop may choose to have the confirmands process out with the choir, clergy, and others.

We sing a closing hymn while the priests, bishop, acolytes, and choir process out.

A priest or deacon will say, "Let us go forth into the world rejoicing in the power of the Spirit." We all respond—and try to do this as strongly as you spoke after the promises were made—

Thanks be to God!

Memories of the Bishop's Visit

Calendar Date

Date in the Liturgical Year (Saint's Day, Pentecost, etc.)

Name of Bishop

Diocese/Episcopacy

Reason for Visitation

Bishop's Signature

Answer Key

First Things First—
(Fill in the blank) JESUS

Names for Jesus—Word Search Puzzle

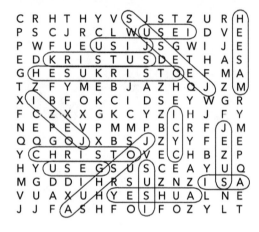

Following Jesus—Jesus Now—Matching

Disciple—listen, pray, learn, share, worship, seek peace, follower, learner, pupil, apprentice, adherent

Apostle—listen, pray, learn, teach, worship, seek peace, share, follower, evangelist, witness, companion, teacher

The Early Church—Matching

Mono—One
Ekklesia—Church/The Gathered
Presbyteros—Leader/Presbyter/Priest
Episkopos—Overseer/Bishop
Diakonos—Deacon
Eucharist—Thanksgiving
Alpha—Beginning
Omega—End
Agape—One

Beginnings and Bishops—
Crossword Puzzle

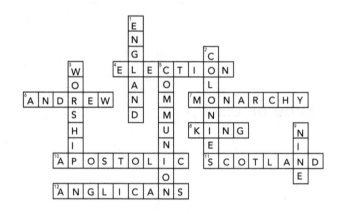

Bishops Who Help Bishops—
Word Search Puzzle

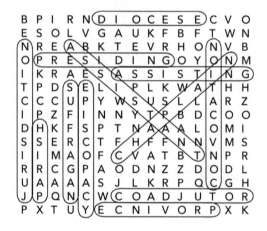

70

Glossary

Anglican Communion: Churches that share a common heritage grounded in Anglican identity; including liturgy and commitment to scripture, tradition, and reason as sources of authority.

Apostle: A term based on the Greek word that means, "someone sent out." The primary New Testament meaning seems to refer to someone who is a personal messenger of Jesus.

Apostolic Age: The earliest period of Christianity, outlined in the book of Acts, beginning with the Great Commission by the resurrected Jesus, and lasting through the death of the last apostle (approximately 33–100 CE).

Apostolic Succession: The belief that bishops are the successors to the apostles and that episcopal authority is derived from the apostles by an unbroken succession in the ministry.

Apse: The area in the church found behind the altar; usually shaped in a semi-circle or polygon accompanied by vaulted ceilings

Bicameral: A governing or legislative body composed of two branches (bi = two, cameral = chambers).

Canon: The written rules that provide a code of laws for the governance of the church; church law.

Cassock: A long, close-fitting garment with narrow sleeves worn by clergy and other ministers. Cassocks are typically black, but also may be blue, gray, or red. Bishops may wear purple cassocks.

Cathedra: Latin, chair with arms; official seat or throne of the bishop in the cathedral of the diocese. The cathedra is considered to be the oldest insignia of the bishop's authority to preside over the church in the diocese.

Chaplain: A person who serves a chapel, or ministers outside a church environment defined by a geographical location. Chaplains serve in a variety of public institutions, including schools, hospitals, and prisons.

Chasuble: The sleeveless outer vestment worn by the celebrant at the Eucharist (picture on page 41).

Chimere: Pronounced *tchuh' meer*. A robe without sleeves worn over an alb or rochet as part of the vestments of a bishop (picture on page 43).

Christian: A follower of Jesus Christ and his teachings.

Cincture: A sash or belt.

Clerical: Of or concerning the clergy. For example, a clerical collar is a collar worn by a member of the clergy.

Congregationalist: The form of church government in which each congregation governs itself and is locally independent and autonomous.

Consecration: To set something or someone apart for a sacred purpose. The central prayer accompanying the laying on of hands in the ordination of bishops, priests, and deacons is called the prayer of consecration.

Cope: A long covering like a cloak or a cape (picture on page 42).

Covenant: A binding and solemn agreement that is freely entered into by two or more parties. A covenant also typically includes terms, oaths, and a ritual enactment.

Crozier: A hooked staff/walking stick carried by a bishop as a symbol of the bishop's office (picture on pages 38 and 55).

Denomination: A large group or confederation of religious congregations organized under a single administrative and legal hierarchy, and united under a common faith and name/title.

Diakonos: Greek for deacon; one whose work in the church is caring for the poor and has charge of distributing money, food, and other goods to the poor.

Diocese: The geographical territory of a diocesan bishop's jurisdiction. The term also refers to the congregations and church members of the diocese.

Discern (or discernment): The activity of determining to make a choice or decision, usually with prayer and the council of others.

Disciple: One who accepts and assists the teachings of another.

Doctrine: From the Latin *docere*, "to teach." Doctrine means teaching or instruction in the most general sense. The word carries the implication of belonging to a school of thought or a body of believers.

Ekklesia: Greek for "assembly," the gathered.

Episcopacy: A system of church governance and supervision by bishops. An episcopacy can be geographical, but the term is used more commonly when referring to dispersed people under the care of a bishop.

Episkopos: Greek for overseer, guardian.

Epistle: A letter; the epistles in the Second Testament are found after the first five books—Matthew, Mark, Luke, John, and Acts.

Examen: The spiritual exercises of St. Ignatius of Loyola (composed from 1522–1524) consisting of a set of Christian mediations, prayers, and mental exercises.

First Testament: The academically preferred term when referring to the part of the Bible that precedes the Second Testament; also known as the Hebrew Testament.

Genesis: Origin, beginning.

General Convention: The church-wide legislative body of The Episcopal Church consisting of the House of Bishops and the House of Deputies. The Convention meets every three years.

Hebrew Testament: The academically preferred term when referring to the part of the Bible that precedes the Second Testament; also known as the First Testament.

House of Bishops: One of the two legislative houses, along with the House of Deputies, that meet during General Convention, composed of all bishops—active and retired—of the church. The House of Bishops meets twice a year during years when General Convention is not scheduled.

House of Deputies: One of the two legislative houses, along with the House of Bishops, that meets during General Convention. The House of Deputies has equal numbers of clergy and lay deputies selected by the dioceses of the Church.

Intention: Conscious or willful purpose to do something. One's intention is freely chosen and not forced.

Jurisdiction: A bishop's authority over an area, typically a diocese, as outlined by the canons of the Church. The diocesan bishop has jurisdiction in his or her diocese. Jurisdiction is not held by bishops coadjutor, suffragan bishops, assisting bishops, resigned bishops, or retired bishops, although they may exercise other episcopal ministries.

Lappet: A decorative flap or loose fold on a hat, headdress, or mitre (picture on pages 41 and 57).

Liturgy: The rites, texts, or patterns that order the church's worship. Liturgy expresses the church's identity and mission. Derived from the Greek words for "people" and "work," sometimes interpreted as "the work of the people."

Ministry: The Christian vocation to serve; one's work as a Christian.

Mission: Christian mission is the sending forth to proclaim the gospel of Jesus Christ in action. From the Latin "to send."

Mission Statement: A formal and public statement about the values and purpose of an organization.

Mitre: The unique headgear worn by a bishop when processing or when giving a blessing (picture on pages 41 and 57).

Monarchy: A state ruled by a monarch, such as a king or queen.

Ordination: A sacramental rite of the Church in which God is asked to give authority and the grace of the Holy Spirit through prayer and the laying on of hands by bishops to those being made bishops, priests, and deacons. The liturgy for ordination can be found in the Book of Common Prayer, pages 860–861.

Pastoral: Concerning the giving of spiritual guidance.

Pectoral Cross: A cross suspended by a chain around the neck which hangs at about the pectoral muscles of the wearer (pictures on pages 38 and 57).

Presbyteros: Greek for elder in a congregation; priest.

Protestant: A denomination that is separate from the Roman Catholic Church; a member or follower of any of the Western Christian churches that are separate from the Roman Catholic Church.

Province: A segment or division of The Episcopal Church. The breakdown of provinces and dioceses can be found on page 29.

Rochet: Pronounced *rah' tcheht*. A vestment of white linen or similar material that replaced the alb and which in time came to be used only by bishops (picture on page 43).

Second Testament: The academically preferred term when referring to the part of the Bible that follows the First, or Hebrew Testament (the Gospels, Acts, and Epistles).

Seniority: A position of privilege and authority earned by reason of longer service.

Stole: Vestment composed of a band of colored cloth worn around the back of the neck and hanging evenly down the front of other vestments (picture on page 42).

The Way: In the Acts of the Apostles (19:9, 22:4, 24:14), the early Christian movement came to be known as "the Way." Jesus' followers were *people of the Way*.

Tippet: A large black scarf worn by clergy over surplice and cassock. It resembles a stole and is worn around the neck with the ends hanging down the front. Emblems such as The Episcopal Church seal or the insignia of the wearer's seminary may ornament it.

Torah: The first five books of the Hebrew Scriptures. In Jewish tradition, the Torah is the most important part of the Hebrew Scriptures for study.

Vestments: The distinctive garments worn by leaders of the Church's worship. Many of the Church's vestments are descended from the ordinary dress of the imperial Roman society in which the early church came into being.

Vision Statement: A description of what an organization would like to achieve or accomplish in the future.

Vocation: From the Latin *vocare*, "to call," vocation may involve a task or job, but it also concerns a way of life, and describes a meaningful approach to work and relationships.

References

Barclay, William. *The Daily Study Bible Series*. Louisville, KY: Westminster John Knox Press, 2001.

Bass, Diana Butler. *A People's History of Christianity: The Other Side of the Story*. New York: HarperCollins, 2010.

The Book of Common Prayer. New York: Church Publishing, 1979.

Canons and Constitution for the Government of The Episcopal Church: Revised by the 2012 General Convention. New York: Church Publishing, 2013.

Gamber, Jenifer. *Your Faith, Your Life: An Invitation to The Episcopal Church*. New York: Morehouse Publishing, 2009.

The Hymnal 1982. New York: Church Publishing, 1985.

Lift Every Voice and Sing II: An African-American Hymnal. New York: Church Publishing, 1993.

Marshall, Paul V. *The Bishop Is Coming! A Practical Guide for Bishops and Congregations*. New York: Church Publishing, 2007.

Odetta. *Odetta: Christmas Spirituals*, performed by Odetta, Vanguard Records, 1994.

Pritchard, Robert W. *History of The Episcopal Church: Revised Edition*. New York: Morehouse Publishing, 1999.

Sullivan, Francis A. *From Apostles to Bishops: The Development of the Episcopacy in the Early Church*. Mahwah, NJ: Paulist Press, 2001.

Wonder, Love, and Praise: A Supplement to The Hymnal 1982. New York: Church Publishing, 1997.

Acknowledgments

I would like to thank

The Most Reverend Frank T. Griswold for his input on theological and liturgical fine points.

The Right Reverend George E. Packard for his support, knowledge, and for never considering "Almy versus Whipple" an appropriate topic for conversation.

The Right Reverend Thomas Ely who generated the idea for the inclusion of "Bishop's Choice" in the Confirmation Booklet.

Sharon Ely Pearson for her vision, support, creativity, and expertise.